Bombs and Bar

To my friend Tony
Hope you enjoy
reading about true
heroes.
Ronald
Oct. 1/22

Also by Ronald Cormier
Les Acadiens et la Seconde Guerre mondiale
The Forgotten Soldiers
Entre bombes et barbelés
"J'ai vécu la guerre"

Bombs and Barbed Wire

Stories of Acadian Airmen and Prisoners of War, 1939-1945

Ronald Cormier

Goose Lane Editions and the Gregg Centre for the Study of War and Society

Edited by Brent Wilson and Barry Norris.
Cover and page design by Julie Scriver.
Cover image: Roger Pichette stands in front of a Fairey Battle, 1941. Collection of the Pichette family.
Printed in Canada by Marquis.
10 9 8 7 6 5 4 3 2 1

Goose Lane Editions acknowledges the generous support of the Government of Canada, the Canada Council for the Arts, and the Government of New Brunswick.

Goose Lane Editions
500 Beaverbrook Court, Suite 330
Fredericton, New Brunswick
CANADA E3B 5X4
gooselane.com

New Brunswick Military History Project
The Brigadier Milton F. Gregg, VC,
Centre for the Study of War and Society
University of New Brunswick
PO Box 4400
Fredericton, New Brunswick
CANADA E3B 5A3
unb.ca/nbmhp

Library and Archives Canada Cataloguing in Publication

Title: Bombs and barbed wire : stories of Acadian airmen and prisoners of war, 1939-1945 / Ronald Cormier.
Other titles: Entre bombes et barbelés. English
Names: Cormier, Ronald, 1946- author. | Gregg Centre for the Study of War and Society, publisher.
Series: New Brunswick military heritage series ; . 29. Description: Series statement: New Brunswick military heritage series ; . 29 | Translation of: Entre bombes et barbelés : témoignages d'aviateurs et de prisonniers de guerre acadiens, 1939-1945. | Includes bibliographical references and index.

Identifiers: Canadiana 20220194645 | ISBN 9781773102788 (softcover)
Subjects: LCSH: World War, 1939-1945,—Prisoners and prisons, German. | LCSH: World War, 1939-1945—Prisoners and prisons, Japanese. | LCSH: World War, 1939-1945—Prisoners and prisons, Canadian. | LCSH: World War, 1939-1945— Aerial operations. | LCSH: World War, 1939-1945 — Maritime Provinces. | LCSH: Acadians—Interviews. Classification: LCC D811.A2 C6813 2022 | DDC 940.4/72—dc23

Goose Lane Editions is located on the unceded territory of the Wəlastəkwiyik whose ancestors along with the Mi'kmaq and Peskotomuhkati Nations signed Peace and Friendship Treaties with the British Crown in the 1700s.

FSC MIX
Paper from responsible sources
www.fsc.org FSC® C103567

To all those young Acadians who gave their lives
in service to Canada during the Second World War

Contents

Introduction

Three generations of Canadians have enjoyed peace and prosperity since the end of the Second World War. This period of our history has contributed to making Canada what it is today. The country is indebted to the more than one million men and women who sacrificed their youth to fight tyranny. Canada remembers them by commemorating the anniversaries of its own participation in the 1939–45 conflict.

Acadians were everywhere Canadians fought in the war, taking part in every theatre of operations where Canada played a significant role. Be it in Italy, northwest Europe, or Hong Kong, there was always an Acadian presence even if it remains little known today. Whether they volunteered at the beginning of the conflict in 1939 or were called to serve later, Acadians did not hesitate to fight on the front lines. They joined the armed forces in the prime of their lives, leaving behind parents, brothers, and sisters, and sometimes wives and young children.

At the time, about 180,000 Acadians lived in the Maritime provinces. Current research allows us to state without hesitation that approximately 24,000 Acadians of military age served in the army, air force, navy, and merchant marine during the war. Some 10,000 of them will have been involved in combat. Acadians took part in the war effort in a proportion similar to that of other ethnic groups in the Maritimes.

The vast majority of Acadians served with the Canadian Army. Hundreds also served with the Royal Canadian Air Force (RCAF) and a few spent the war in the Royal Air Force (RAF), mainly with bomber squadrons. Many might also have served with the Royal Canadian Navy (RCN) because of their links to the sea, but their numbers in the naval service were very low. The RCN was not very friendly to francophones and sometimes even hostile—it was forbidden to speak French on most naval bases.

In an earlier book, *The Forgotten Soldiers*, published in 1990, I told the stories of eighteen Acadian soldiers who valiantly fought in Italy and northwest Europe. A second book, *Entre bombes et barbelés*, published in French in 1990, related the experiences of ten Acadian aviators and prisoners of war. *Bombs and Barbed Wire* is the English language version of that book. It has been expanded to include the story of a young airman from Edmundston, Henri Édouard Dubé, who did not return from the war. I describe his journey from his personnel file held at Library and Archives Canada in Ottawa and other information garnered from the internet. The other accounts are based on in-person, recorded interviews in French with veterans during the summer of 1989. I then transcribed the interviews and translated them into English. What appears in this book represents between 30 and 50 percent of the interviews. As such, the words are theirs; I have altered only certain sentences for clarity. All of the veterans have now passed away.

The first half of this book focuses on the experiences of Acadian airmen serving with the RCAF over western Europe, while the remainder chronicles the exploits of Acadian soldiers fighting in different theatres of operations with the Canadian Army. War in the air offers a different perspective on the conflict. Dropping bombs from 3,000 or 5,000 metres above a target on the ground is an anonymous undertaking. Airmen never get a close look at the destruction they have sown from the sky. They never have personal contact with the enemy. When an airman or soldier goes into combat, he foresees the possibility of being wounded or killed. Few imagine they might be captured by the enemy. This is what happened to six of the men in this book. Their experiences in prisoner of war (POW) camps varied greatly depending on whether they were taken by the Germans or by the Japanese. Those held in Germany or in occupied European countries lived through difficult, often arduous, times, especially as the end of the war neared in 1945. Those captured in the fall of Hong Kong on Christmas Day 1941 were treated like slaves of the Empire of the Rising Sun, which gave little importance to the survival of its victims.

I thank the ten veterans who agreed to let me relate their experiences and sufferings. One of the participants (John Arsenault) in the original French-language version wanted to remain anonymous. His family has given us permission to use his name in this edition.

Blair Bourgeois wears the insignia of a wireless
air gunner (WAG) on his RCAF uniform.

Collection of Mrs. Germaine Bourgeois

Chapter One

A Different Life
The Story of Blair Bourgeois

Sixty missions: the number of sorties in Blair Bourgeois's RCAF logbook at the end of the Second World War. When war broke out in Europe in September 1939, Bourgeois was only eighteen years old and had just completed high school in his hometown of Moncton, New Brunswick. He was an athlete and member of the pre-war militia. "I was in the non-permanent militia and they came to get me to join the army. At the time, one had to sign up for active duty. I refused. I spent the winter playing hockey with a team made up of different regiments like the New Brunswick Rangers and the Saint John Fusiliers." Bourgeois's decision not to enlist had nothing to do with his lack of patriotism, quite to the contrary. "I had always wanted to join the air force. I told myself I wanted to be a flyer. In the spring [1940], I quit the militia to enlist in the air force. I had a good friend with whom I had played baseball, and he's the one who made it possible for me to join. I was nineteen."

The young man's enthusiasm for flying was slow to become reality.

They weren't ready for us who would train for what we called "aircrew" and we had to do guard duty for three or four months before starting our training in Toronto (No. 1 Manning Depot). After that, I went to Calgary, in Alberta (No. 2 Wireless School)

Most RCAF bomber bases in England were in Yorkshire. Nos. 408 and 427 Squadrons were at Leeming, No. 425 Squadron at Dishforth, then at Tholthorpe, and No. 423 Squadron at East Moor. Ronald Cormier / Mike Bechthold

and to Moose Jaw (No. 32 Service Flying Training School) in Saskatchewan. I did my training as a wireless air gunner. I finally passed my exams and got my wings. After that, they formed crews to be sent to England.

Like all new aircrew arriving from Canada in 1941, Bourgeois had to complete his training at an Operational Training Unit (OTU) before joining No. 408 Squadron of the RCAF at Balderton, in Nottinghamshire. This unit, formed on June 24, 1941, was the second Canadian bomber squadron created in England. Canadian units were part of the RAF's Bomber Command: "No. 408 was a Canadian squadron in No. 5 Group of the Royal Air Force. In Squadron 408, there was a mixture of Canadians and flyers from other countries."

It was in a Hampden bomber that Bourgeois, as a wireless air gunner, embarked on his first mission on April 21, 1942, months after arriving in England. "On our first sortie, we dropped mines near Terschelling, an island in the North Sea. The objective was to blow up German ships which left the ports in that area." In his baptism by fire, his bomber became the target of enemy anti-aircraft defences.

The first sortie, it's all new.... Projectors shone cones of light to be able to shoot at us. With 408 Squadron, it was mostly mine-laying operations. They were the worst of all because we had to go down to 500 feet in bays full of enemy ships. When I went on a mission, I didn't know if I'd return or not. When we left with a full load of bombs, the aircraft took a long time to take off. The wheels left the ground and hit it again, bounced and hit again until we had enough speed to climb. We had to reach 500 feet to jump with a parachute. When you were above 500 feet, you told yourself that you could bail out if anything happened.

All squadron bombers took off one behind the other. Each aircraft had its arrival time over the target. Be it Berlin or another city, we had to be there on time. When we crossed the coast of England, we were anxious to get to the other side. If we had to

A Handley Page Hampden Mk. 1 bomber from No. 408 Squadron, RCAF, in England in July 1941. It carried about two tonnes of bombs and had a range of 1,800 kilometres. Library and Archives Canada/ PA-1447744

bail out, it would at least be over land and not into the North Sea. We didn't fly in a straight line to the target. We made our way to a point and then headed towards the objective while losing altitude to gain a bit of speed. When we crossed over the target, we were flying as fast as possible to avoid German anti-aircraft fire. The bombardier told the pilot to go left or right to drop our bombs on target because the winds pushed the plane from side to side. Once the bomber dropped its load, we had to take a photo. It took us a minute or two. It was more unnerving because we had to fly in a straight line over the target. We couldn't take evasive action to avoid the flak. The German batteries detected the noise of our plane's engines and directed their fire against us. Flak came up like clouds and exploded. When you were flying in a straight line, with the flak exploding in front of the plane, it wasn't funny.

At the beginning, we only went out on moonlit nights because we could see better. The German fighters could also see us better and came up to shoot us down. At this time, we didn't have any days off. We had to be there every night. After a while, we stopped going out when the moon was full except for special operations. I lost friends when I was on Hampdens with 408. We lost six crews during sorties in which I didn't take part for one reason or another. When they didn't return, I just told myself they're gone, that's it. It was a different life.

On the night of May 30-31, 1942, less than six weeks after Bourgeois went on his first sortie with 408 Squadron, he took part in the first thousand-bomber raid by Bomber Command. The objective was Cologne, on the Rhine River. "In this raid against Cologne, we were caught in what we called a stabilized yaw. We were at 12,000 feet and lost control of the aircraft. We got ready to bail out, but, fortunately, the pilot managed to regain control at 500 feet, the minimum height for jumping. When we got back to base, we counted 250 flak holes in the plane." Luck had smiled on the crew, which returned to Balderton and undertook other missions. Bourgeois flew fifteen more sorties with 408 Squadron, which took him over Lorient in France, and Bremen, Emden, Duisburg, and Düsseldorf in Germany.

At the end of June 1942, the RCAF created a new squadron in Britain. The unit, No. 425 "Alouette" Squadron, was the first to group mainly French-speaking Canadians serving in existing RCAF squadrons and in the RAF. Bourgeois was called upon to join the squadron's ranks in Dishforth, Yorkshire. With fifteen sorties in his logbook, he had considerable experience.

I arrived at 425 Squadron on August 18, 1942. We were three French Canadians from 408 Squadron.... I got my pilot officer's commission when I was with 425. We flew Wellingtons. They were better than Hampdens because the planes were new. When I got to 425, the guys had no experience. It took about a month to a month and a half before we did our first trip.[1] There were other Acadians with 425, mostly mechanics and ground crews.

---

1   No. 425 Squadron's first raid was against Aachen in western Germany.

I got along well with the guys in the ground crews. I always believed that we had to take care of them because they were the ones taking care of our planes. These guys had to be back at base before midnight. Us, we could return when we wanted. We often brought back beer for them on Saturday nights. We hid it in our long coats. The guys greatly appreciated it. Life was good at Dishforth. It was an old base from before the war with nice rooms. I had my own room and a batman. He brought me tea and all that. It was a nice place.... I liked it.

Bourgeois flew sixteen sorties with "Alouette" Squadron. Two of them remained vivid in his memory.

Our first bombing run was on October 5, 1942. Our commanding officer was Wing Commander St-Pierre.[2] The hardest sortie of all was on the evening of my birthday [December 31] in 1942. We attacked Brest, in France, where there were two German warships, the *Gneisenau* and the *Scharnhorst*. We had to go down to 500 feet and fly over the harbour. It was very dark that night and the thought of having to wait for the guns to open up was very unnerving. It was the worst raid of all.

One night, returning to the coast of England after a raid against Essen, we were 150 miles off course. Those bombers didn't fly very fast, only 110 or 120 miles per hour, maybe 150 with a tail wind. One of my friends had come to visit me at the base. Since they had no news of us after an hour, they assumed we had been lost. When a guy went missing, the padre came with the military police to collect his personal belongings. My friend was about to return to his base with my camera when someone ran up to tell him I was okay.

---

2   Wing Commander J.M.W. St-Pierre commanded No. 425 Squadron from June 25, 1942, to September 30, 1943.

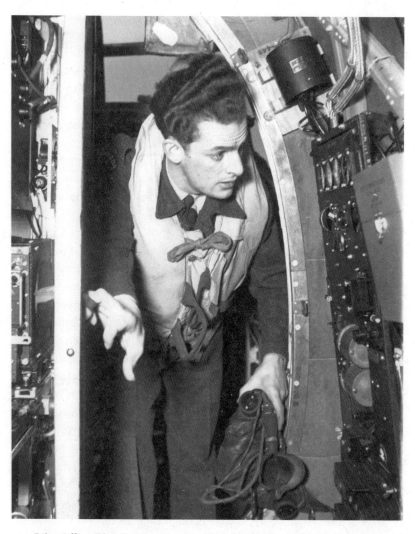

Pilot Officer Blair Bourgeois makes his way from the cockpit to the bomb bay of a Wellington bomber of No. 425 Squadron in Dishforth, February 16, 1943. DND/RCAF Photo Unit, PL-15442

Officers who did not have flying duty had a hard time imagining what it could be like on a raid. Contrary to orders, some managed to experience war in the air. Bourgeois remembered that their first sortie was usually their last because a bomber was not built for passengers. "Our squadron doctor, Doctor Payette, a small man, kept asking us to go on a raid with us. We weren't supposed to do that, but one night we took him along. We were caught in the beams of searchlights and flak. He was so scared that he fainted. We laid him down and tied him to a small cot in the plane. He didn't come back on another raid after that."

The success of a sortie against a target in enemy territory, some 800 or more kilometres from base, depended on many factors. Some were beyond the control of the men in the aircraft. The fate of an aircrew relied largely on the expertise of those on the ground.

When the meteorologists made mistakes about conditions over the target during daytime raids, consequences could be very bad. If we were flying in clouds at 500 or 1,000 feet and the clouds disappeared when we neared the city to be bombed, we were naked against German fighters waiting for us. It wasn't funny. When this happened, we tried to hide in the clouds. When told to go somewhere, the British of the RAF went whether it was cloudy or not and were shot down. I was scared but I told myself that I was going, that's it, that's all. During the five or six hours of a flight, I had to be on my toes all the time. A moment of distraction by a crew member could lead to our loss. We never knew when a German fighter was behind us. If the guys chatted or joked around and the tail gunner told us there was a German fighter coming, we probably would not have heard him. When the guys started joking around, I told them to wait until we got back to base before laughing. We'd have enough time for that while having a drink at the pub. I'm sure some of my friends didn't come back because of a lack of attention in the air.

Like many other airmen, Bourgeois believed that luck couldn't be left to chance alone. The odds had to be put in one's favour by all means possible.

I was always very good at finding four-leaf clovers. It was rare that I couldn't find one before taking off. We checked out our bomber at dispersal before climbing in. There was grass around the plane and I was always able to find a four-leaf clover. I brought one on the plane almost every time. I had a small doll my mother had brought me from Chicago, I think. I put it in a sort of small round box in my room and after every raid I drew a small bomb on it. There were sixty at the end. My first tour of duty was thirty sorties. The second one was twenty trips. My first tour took nearly a year because we couldn't go out in bad weather.

Bourgeois's first tour of operations ended with his thirty-first sortie while with "Alouette" Squadron. The experience gained landed him a posting as signals officer with an OTU in August 1943. He briefed crews who had to familiarize themselves with new types of bombers. This assignment allowed him to get away from the constant tension of bombing raids. The next time Bourgeois climbed aboard a bomber, it was a Sterling of the RAF's 199 Squadron, stationed at North Creake, northeast of London, where he arrived on August 18, 1943. He took part in his last operation four months later on December 18.

I flew twenty-nine sorties with 199 Squadron. It was a special operations unit. We dropped things to jam enemy radar [aluminum strips called "window"] and flares to light up the target. This was before they had Pathfinder[3] squadrons. We also dropped phosphorescent bombs to set fire to the objective. With 199 Squadron, I went on thirteen special operations in fifteen days. I drew small pictures in my logbook to say what kind of raid we

---

3   Pathfinders were specialized units of aircraft sent ahead of the main force to mark and illuminate targets.

had been on. We weren't supposed to do that in case our logbook fell into enemy hands.

As a Canadian air force officer, Bourgeois had opportunities that most of his compatriots did not have at a time when everything was rationed. He also had something few other Canadian aviators enjoyed: a car.

I had bought a car for cheap, a Triumph, a sports car. I kept it until three days before I returned to Canada. When I sold it, it had seen better days. I even sold it for more than I had paid! I didn't have much trouble getting gas. I managed. Most of the gas stations were run by women because the men were off to war. Officers got ration coupons to purchase material for uniforms. Since I had a lot more coupons than I needed, I went to see those women and traded them for gas. I had room for three gas cans behind the seat. That way, I always had some. Every month we got a gas ration good for driving 150 miles. My friends who had cars would put them up on blocks when they had burned their ration. That wasn't the case for me.

I was well received by the British. I met people who were well off. They owned a large factory. They invited me to dinner many times and we became friends. At the time, lighters were scarce in England. I wrote to my mother asking to send me a nice one. She bought one with a cigarette case. I gave it to them as a gift. Farmers who had less than six chickens didn't have to declare their egg production. To get food, I went to see them and gave them ration coupons or cigarettes my mother sent from Canada. They gave me eggs in return. Some men lost their lives just to have an egg. Before leaving on a sortie and when we returned, we were given what we called a "flying meal," an egg and bacon. I saw guys who were not scheduled to go on a raid volunteer to replace someone who was absent in order to get his meal. Many didn't return from these raids.

Near the end of the war, Allied domination of the skies over Germany allowed bombers to attack all sorts of targets. Many aircrew questioned the morality of Bomber Command in attacking certain objectives. "I remember guys saying that we shouldn't bomb historic buildings. When you are flying at 15,000 or 18,000 feet and they're shooting at you, you just want to drop your bombs and head back to base. We didn't think of the people who were victims of our bombs because we had to think of other things like enemy fighter and flak."

When the war in Europe ended in May 1945, Bourgeois was already back in Canada, having returned earlier that year. He was demobilized in the summer of 1945 with the rank of flight lieutenant. "I think I was the first Acadian from Moncton to become an officer and to take part in bombing raids. At the time French Canadians had a hard time because they were French speaking." Bourgeois's observation probably explains why, despite his sixty sorties, he was never awarded the Distinguished Flying Cross (DFC) or Distinguished Flying Medal (DFM), as were many of his contemporaries who logged a lot fewer hours in combat.

When he returned to Canada, Blair Bourgeois went to play baseball in Quebec. He became a lumber salesman in Mont-St-Hilaire and in 1948 married Germaine Richard from Cap-de-Richibouctou, New Brunswick. They had two daughters and returned to Moncton when he retired in 1978.

Roger Pichette proudly wears the uniform of an air gunner (AG)
of the RCAF in a photo probably taken before he left for England.

Collection of the Pichette family

Chapter Two

A Bloody Colonial
The Story of Roger Pichette

Every young man who flew on bombing raids with the Royal Canadian Air Force in the Second World War experienced similarities and differences throughout the war. They seldom saw their adversary up close and did not witness the whirlwind they dropped from the skies. Roger Pichette, like his fellow Acadian, Blair Bourgeois, served in the RCAF at about the same time and flew similar kinds of missions as a sergeant and tail gunner. Pichette, however, received the DFM and later became involved in recruiting and promoting the war effort, and then served as an instructor.

Pichette was only two years old when his parents moved from Chandler, on the Gaspé Peninsula in Quebec, to Campbellton, New Brunswick. He spent his youth in this northern town before leaving to pursue classical studies at the seminary in St-Hyacinthe, Quebec in the mid-1930s. His schooling made him choose the RCAF instead of the army.

The period of history preceding the Second World War was marked by the rise of totalitarian regimes in Europe. From the mid-1930s, Stalin, the communist leader, was the absolute master of the Soviet Union. At the other end of the political spectrum, nationalists and the extreme right had taken power. Fascism reigned in Italy under Mussolini since 1925, and in Germany Hitler and the Nazis gained power and eliminated all opposition in 1933. It was a turbulent time that fascinated Pichette.

For three or four years at the seminary, I had a professor, Father Joseph Lefebvre, who had a doctorate in history. That was rare at the time. He taught biblical history and, during courses, he took about fifteen minutes to talk about "isms": communism, Nazism, socialism, and capitalism. In 1937-1938, he began to tell us about Hitler and Nazism. For example, he explained what was going on in Czechoslovakia.[4] The subject fascinated me, and I often stayed after class to ask questions. I was fifteen or sixteen then. I told my classmates I thought we would have another war and wanted to go if I was old enough. They told me: "Pichette, you'll take to the woods with us." I was sure there would be a war. I had read lots of books on the First War. I knew the story of Vimy, the Somme, trenches, mud, gas, and all that. That probably explains why I chose the air force. I didn't want to know the misery soldiers had endured during the 14-18 war.

At the end of classes on June 6, 1940, nineteen-year-old Pichette enlisted in the RCAF. He took an informed decision at the right time.

The Canadian government had set up the British Commonwealth [Air] Training Plan and had begun recruiting. To join the air force, one needed to have finished high school. My classical studies were worth a bit more than high school. I enlisted in Quebec City[5] because my grandmother Rousseau knew Captain Ivers, who had served in the First World War. Ivers knew Flight Lieutenant Gerry Monahan, who was the recruiting officer there. I had connections but I still had to fill in the required forms and

---

4   Without the consent of the Czech government, Britain, France, Italy, and Germany signed the Munich Agreement in September 1938, allowing Hitler to annex the Sudetenland, a part of Czechoslovakia with a large population of German origin. Hitler invaded what was left of Czechoslovakia in May 1939.

5   No. 4 Manning Depot was in Quebec City.

pass the medical. That's how I left Quebec City with about fifteen men of English or Irish descent, with names like MacWilliam, Blackmore, Kelly, Delaney, and one of Greek ancestry. I think I was the only francophone in the group. From Quebec City we went to No. 1 Manning Depot in Toronto for basic training. That's where we got our uniforms and boots. We drilled every day. After a month, they sent us to No. 1 Initial Training School at the Eglinton Club, an equestrian club in Toronto. Our barracks smelled like a barn. We used the tennis courts to drill.

We spent about four hours a day in class. We were about two hundred in all, except for a few who wanted to become navigators, hoped to become pilots. A week before the end of our course, we were paraded before an officer for an interview to decide what we'd be doing. The officer asked me to give him three choices. "What is your first choice?" he said. I answered: "Pilot." He wrote down pilot on a sheet of paper.

Pichette gave the same answer for his two other choices.

Today I realize that I had no chance of becoming a pilot because of my answers. When the list of our postings came out, about a hundred men and I were sent to No. 1 Wireless School in Montreal, the school for radio operators. After finishing the courses in Montreal, I went to Jarvis, Ontario, to the No. 1 Bombing and Gunnery School. I crossed to England in February 1941 on a troop transport, the *Georgic*.[6] We were only a few aviators amongst a throng of soldiers. Arriving in Gourock, Scotland, we were sent to different OTUs. I went to No. 1 OTU in Basingborne, near Cambridge.

On June 11, 1941, Pichette was posted to an RAF bomber squadron. No. 142 Squadron had a long history, having been formed in Egypt in

---

6   The *Georgic* left Halifax unescorted on February 24, 1941.

February 1918. At the onset of the Second World War, the unit saw combat on the continent. It served in France flying Fairey Battles, single-engine light bombers, as part of No. 1 Group of the RAF.

I was stationed with 142 Squadron at Binbrook, not far from Grimsby, on the Humber River in Lincolnshire. They called us Canadians "bloody Colonials." We were less disciplined than the British. Officers didn't scare us even though we were only sergeants. It was quite rare at the time to be commissioned at the end of one's training. The few officers were old men of the Royal Air Force from before the war, guys from thirty to thirty-two years old. Our bomber was a Wimpy, a Wellington Mark 1c, with Rolls-Royce Merlin engines. Those engines didn't produce much power, and we needed all of the runway to take off with our bomb load. They were the first types of Wellingtons, and the engines were known for their oil leaks. We later got more power-ful engines, Pratt and Whitney and Hercules. The port of Hull [Kingston upon Hull] was not far from our base. It was protected by barrage balloons, which we didn't like because there was a lot of fog in the area. We had to avoid making too wide a circuit when landing because we could hit the balloons to which were attached steel cables to shear off aircraft wings. The pilot of my first crew was Tom Parker, a guy from Winnipeg. Our co-pilot was a Scotsman, Willie Caldow, the navigator was Fred Gauley from Toronto, the wireless air gunner was an Englishman named Phillips, the nose gunner Brian Thomas came from Wales, and I was tail gunner.

It was with this Anglo-Canadian crew that Pichette flew his first sortie in May 1941. "Our first raid was against Lyon in France. It was what they called a 'nickel raid.' We dropped leaflets. We didn't have any bombs. We were seeing anti-aircraft fire for the first time as we crossed the coast of France. There was always the risk of being attacked by a night fighter but there was less anti-aircraft fire than elsewhere. We were gone for five and

Roger Pichette at the Bombing and Gunnery School in Jarvis, Ontario, at the beginning of 1941. He is standing in front of a Fairey Battle, the type of aircraft on which he trained. Collection of the Pichette family

a half hours. It was to give us experience. We said it was 'a piece of cake.' At the time, raids like that were quite rare."

His baptism by fire was probably the easiest raid of all during his twenty months with 142 Squadron. Other sorties took him over the most heavily defended areas of Germany. "The Germans had four thousand anti-aircraft guns to protect the Krupp industries and the cities of Essen, Dortmund, Düsseldorf, and Duisburg in the Ruhr Valley. When the intelligence officers asked us after our return from a raid if there had been a lot of flak, we replied ironically that we had lowered our landing gear and taxied over the target."

Pichette didn't think of joking when he came back from one raid against the Krupp works in Essen. As the tail gunner, he occupied the most vulnerable position in the bomber.

At the beginning of August 1941,[7] we went on a night raid against Essen. In the rear turret, I had an oxygen mask with an intercom to talk to the others. At 10,000 feet, I'd set the oxygen for 15,000 feet and kept the flow for 5,000 higher than we were flying. A Wellington loaded with bombs didn't climb very fast. For Essen, we climbed as high as possible, which was about 18,000 feet. That night we were hit by anti-aircraft fire. I was tossed about in the rear. It was quite bad and Tom Parker began calling me. I didn't reply. I had passed out because a piece of shrapnel had cut my oxygen line. It had also cut my communications. Tom Parker sent someone back to see what was going on. Fortunately, my turret was centred and they managed to open the doors to help me. This incident was reported when we landed. I had to see the doctor, who questioned me. I told him I hadn't fallen asleep over Essen. I then told the doctor that I had suffered from stomach problems for the past two or three months. He decided to send me to hospital for tests. I was absent from the squadron for a few weeks. When I came back, Tom Parker had found a new tail gunner to take my place.

This change probably saved Pichette's life because Tom Parker's crew ran out of luck on the night of October 21/22, 1941. "Tom's bomber was shot down during a raid against Bremen. The crew was buried in Wilhelmshaven[8] in Germany." The loss of his former crew, especially Flight Sergeant Parker, touched him deeply. For him Parker was much more than a crewmate.

In 1941 and 1942, out of every bomber crew who began a tour of thirty operations, only ten made it to the end. The law of averages was often the subject of conversations in the mess. A lot of guys I

---

7   According to the *Bomber Command War Diaries 1939-1945*, this raid took place on the night of August 6/7, 1942. Three of the 106 bombers taking part were lost.

8   According to documents from the Air Historical Branch of the UK Ministry of Defence, Flight Sergeant Parker, and Sergeants Gauley, Thomas, and Sharing were buried in the British military cemetery at Oldenburg, near Wilhelmshaven. The bodies of Flight Sergeant Phillips and Sergeant Forrest were never recovered after their bomber went missing over the North Sea.

knew well were lost. It took time to forget them. In Grimsby, there was a skating rink. Near there was a Canadian squadron patrolling the coast with Hudson aircraft.[9] We played hockey against their team. Tom Parker played centre and I played defence. We had problems with our team because we often lost players. The Coastal Command team had good players and seldom lost men.

Sergeant Pichette's new crew after leaving hospital was not entirely unfamiliar to him. His former co-pilot, Willie Caldow, was now at the controls of the Wellington X. "I went with Willie Caldow and a new crew. Our navigator was a New Zealander, Percy Stewart, and the nose gunner was named Straffen. It's funny but I don't remember the names of the others..." It was with this crew that Pichette flew the majority of his thirty-eight sorties. In the fall of 1941, the RAF's Bomber Command was alone in taking the air war to Germany and the occupied countries since the United States had not yet entered the war.

We went on a raid against Berlin. It took us eight hours and ten minutes. We were afraid of running out of fuel. A raid against Hamburg or Kiel took more than six hours. We flew for about five hours to attack the Ruhr Valley. In 1941, we went on a bombing mission against ports on the Baltic: Lübeck, Stettin, and Kiel. Those trips were very long and the ports well protected. When we attacked targets in Germany, like Essen or Duisburg, we dropped our bombs even if we didn't see the Krupp works, the hell with it.

One time we took off to bomb Essen. Our meteorologists had told us the weather would be nice. When we arrived over the Ruhr Valley, we were caught in an electrical storm. The antenna trailing behind the plane and my four Browning machine guns seemed surrounded by flames. I was getting worried. The plane was shaking so much that it was like being on a horse in a rodeo. I called the pilot and said with a shaky voice: "Willie, my machine

---

9   No. 407 Squadron, stationed at North Coates, was part of Coastal Command which patrolled at sea.

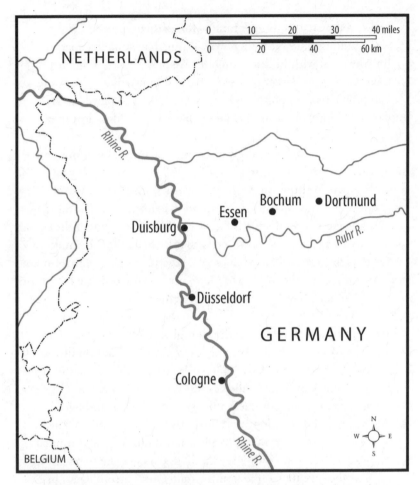

The Ruhr River Valley was the target of most Allied air raids during the Second World War. The Krupp works were in Essen. Ronald Cormier/ Mike Bechthold

guns are on fire, the antenna is on fire." Willie replied, imitating my trembling voice: "Roger, my props are on fire." Everything seemed on fire. It was static electricity. I was sure there weren't any damn German fighters around. We dropped our bombs and headed back to England. We had lost our compass, we were lost.

The only thing we knew was that we were over the Ruhr Valley. When we came out of the storm, we were over the Zuiderzee in northern Holland.

They found their way back to their base at Grimsby, and continued flying numerous other sorties only to face other perils.

I nearly froze my toes one winter night when electricity failed in my heated flying boots. After that I wore Eskimo boots and good woollen socks. At 15,000 feet in winter, the temperature could drop to minus 30 or 40 degrees Fahrenheit. I took part in thirty-eight sorties and only three of them involved searches at sea or mine laying. Of those thirty-eight missions, I went to Essen seven times on raids against the Krupp works in twenty months.

Of his thirty-eight sorties, certain ones were memorable because of their spectacular aspect. One of them earned Sergeant Pichette and his pilot, Willie Caldow, the DFM.

The raid for which I was decorated happened in February 1942, but the story begins well before that. We had been invited to dinner for Christmas [1941] by a family near our base, but two or three days before, our squadron was put on alert. The large German warships — *Scharnhorst*, *Gneisenau*, and *Prinz Eugen* — which were in Brest, France, were supposed to try to escape through the English Channel. We even trained on Christmas Day just in case they tried. We spent most of Christmas Day playing cards in our flying suits. At the beginning of January 1942 [on the 6th] our target was Brest....Our co-pilot was Ted Spicer, who was going out on one of his first sorties. That night, we were hit by anti-aircraft fire. Spicer, who was in the observer's position and not up front as co-pilot, was wounded in the left arm. All I heard on my headset was: "Hit, Ted has been hit." I knew things weren't going well when I lost communications.

The navigator applied a tourniquet to Ted's arm. Instead of returning to Grimsby, we landed in southern England where there was a Canadian fighter squadron. They took Ted to the hospital and when they cut open his tunic, his arm fell out. He ended his career in control towers.

Six weeks later, the *Kriegsmarine* decided that the time was ripe for the three cruisers to risk the passage of the English Channel. They left Brest at 2300 hours on February 11, and followed the French coast at the high speed of 27 knots. They hoped to stay undetected by Britain's air force or navy. They were covered by German fighters based on the Channel coast in France.

On February 12, the German ships entered the English Channel. We left Grimsby and flew down to Dover and then went searching for them off the coast of Belgium. The weather was bad that day. Cloud cover descended to 500 or 1,000 feet. We were flying two by two and were not in formation. When we came out of the clouds we saw the "Chicago pianos," the anti-aircraft guns on the ships. I don't know how we made it through that. Our bomber, with Willie Caldow at the controls, was loaded with armour-piercing bombs, which should have been dropped from 6,000 or 10,000 feet. We had to drop them from 1,000 feet. And then that's when I saw, with my own eyes, my first huge swastika, which was flying on the *Scharnhorst*. We dropped our bombs on the *Prinz Eugen*, which was ahead of the *Scharnhorst* and the *Gneisenau*. It's hard to say if we hit the ship or not. It seems we were lucky and our bombs hit the *Prinz Eugen*,[10] but at the altitude from which we let them go, they didn't do enough damage to sink it. Even if the bombs exploded, the damage would have only been superficial because they didn't penetrate the ship.

---

10   According to the No. 142 Squadron journal: "In spite of intense flak and fighter opposition, two of the Wellingtons pressed home their attack, dropping their bombs on the warships." (Documents provided to the author by the Air Historical Branch of the UK Ministry of Defence.)

We were attacked by Focke-Wulf and Messerschmitt fighters. There were an incredible number of German planes around those ships. Paddy Richardson, a young Canadian, was with us for his first trip. He was in the observer's position in the centre of the plane. He saw a lot of action that day! He was well initiated. Even if it was mid-February, I had sweated a lot and had fired I don't know how many rounds. All the smoke and the cordite had stuck to my face. I was all black. That was the most difficult raid for us. I'll never forget that afternoon.

The following October 28, the RAF acknowledged Pichette, who now held the rank of flight sergeant, by awarding him the DFM, but the honour would be presented to him only a few months later, after his return to Canada.

A second raid remained vivid in his memory for totally different reasons. This sortie took place on the night of March 3/4, 1942, less than three weeks after the attack against the German cruisers off the coast of Belgium.

One of my last raids was probably the easiest. Our target was the Renault factories near Paris [in Billancourt]. These plants worked for the German war effort. It was understood that, when we bombed an occupied country, we had to hit the objective. We crossed France at low altitude, between 1,000 and 1,500 feet. When we flew over villages, I could see people opening their doors to look and I could see lights. We had 8,000 pounds of bombs and were in the last wave, the last to arrive over the target. Arriving in Paris, we didn't have any problem making out our objective because everything was on fire along the Seine except at the end where there were large tanks. We climbed to 4,000 or 5,000 feet and dropped our bombs on those reservoirs. We hit them. From my position in the tail, I saw their covers rise 800 or 900 feet in the air. Flames erupted. The bomber began shaking from the force of the explosions. We had seen a real fire and a target that had really been hit. You told yourself that it was all worthwhile.

When we went on raids to France, we filled the plane's cot with thousands of propaganda leaflets. When we dropped them, they fell all over the place. That evening, they read: "Tonight, we bombed the Renault works. Tomorrow?" We asked civilians to evacuate the areas around French factories working for the Germans. When we finished bombing, we weren't far from the Eiffel Tower. We descended to 600 or 700 feet and flew circuits around it. All of a sudden, our navigator, Percy Stewart, noticed we hadn't dropped our leaflets. We were supposed to drop them further east, towards Lyon, and not on Paris. We headed east and Paddy Richardson, our wireless operator, and Percy Stewart threw them out of the plane. On our return trip, our pilot, Willie Caldow was singing *La Marseillaise*. We had forgotten that our commanding officer, Wing Commander Simmons, was also on the raid. Our crew was one of the most experienced in the squadron.

All bombers had been back at the base for some time before we landed. All the guys said it had been "a piece of cake." Those with less experience had found it easy and the veterans had seen little flak. Our Wimpy hadn't come back. The men wondered what could have happened to Willie Caldow and his crew. We landed about twenty minutes after the others. The guys had a lot of questions. They wanted to know why we were late. We explained that we had forgotten to drop our leaflets and that we had headed east to drop them, that we were the last over the objective, that we had circled the target but we failed to mention our circuits of the Eiffel Tower. The intelligence officers asked all sorts of questions. When we were done, Paddy Richardson, who hadn't said a word, told the officer who wanted to know if we had dropped our leaflets: "No, we delivered them door to door." The officer quickly understood that we had done a bit of tourism. That explained our late arrival.

Roger Pichette and his crewmates from No. 142 Squadron RAF (left to right):
Sergeant Percy Stewart (RAF); Sergeant Willie Caldow (RAF), pilot;
Sergeant Ted Spicer (Royal New Zealand Air Force);
Sergeant James Straffen (RAF); Sergeant Roger Pichette (RCAF);
and Sergeant Stanley Oertel (RAF). Collection of the Pichette family

Some 236 bombers took part in the raid against the Renault works. At the time, it was an impressive number of aircraft. At the end of May, however, the destruction raining from the skies took on a whole new dimension. Pichette participated in the first thousand-bomber raid by Bomber Command on the night of May 30/31 against a familiar target. "I remember that, in May 1941, we had gone on a raid against Cologne, what they called a maximum effort. We were 120 bombers at the most, including a dozen from our squadron. A year later, we went one thousand at a time. We followed the Rhine River and in the bright moonlight we could see the city with its big cathedral."

Mounting these thousand-bomber raids required more coordination to get the desired results from such a concentration of aircraft. All had to follow one another in a stream that could stretch for twenty or thirty kilometres, and drop their bombs on the designated target. The first over the objective could see it clearly, but once the bombing began the target disappeared in smoke. And where there were clouds, it was hidden even from the first who arrived. It was with the aim of solving both of those problems and improving precision that the RAF created specialized units, the Pathfinders, to act as spotters for the others.

> We were part of the Pathfinders for a while. We carried incendiary bombs and flares to mark the target. We were the first over the objective. The Germans lit fires in fields about fifty miles from the target to try to fool the bombers heading to their objective. The danger was double for the Pathfinders because we were the first over the target and we spent a lot more time there than the others. We were more exposed to flak. Sometimes we had to stay to drop other markers or take photos. We flew at 12,000 or 14,000 feet and the other bombers could be at 18,000 or 20,000 feet. Some Pathfinders were hit by bombs dropped from above.

Pichette completed thirty-four sorties with No. 142 Squadron between June 11, 1941, and August 11, 1942. He was promoted to the rank of pilot officer eleven days before leaving. Three weeks later, he was recommended for the DFM. Even though he was now an officer, the award was for his service when he was a sergeant.[11] The recommendation from his superiors read: "On all occasions his devotion to duty and his supreme coolness in the face of the toughest enemy defences have proved an inspiration to all."[12] He was awarded the medal on October 6.

Pichette completed four more missions before the end of his service with 142 Squadron. This number did not include the numerous training flights all crews had to undertake. Between raids and training, Pichette was given free time and leave. When he arrived in England in 1941 he visited London, but that attraction didn't last long.

> It was still the time of the famous German night raids. We learned, after a few trips to London, that it wasn't the ideal place to spend a weekend. You spent your time in the Underground. One time I went to King's Cross station to take my train on a

---

11   The DFM was awarded to non-commissioned officers, the DFC to officers.

12   Information provided to the author by the UK Ministry of Defence.

Monday morning. I was told that the station had been bombed and that I had to go elsewhere for my train. With all the problems with transportation, one risked getting back to base late.

I went at least a year before going back to London.

At the beginning of 1942, No. 142 Squadron left for Blida, in North Africa, but Pichette was no longer with the unit. The stress of life as a tail gunner, the most vulnerable position in a bomber, caused him health problems. "I returned to Canada in December 1942. I had stomach ulcers. I crossed to New York on the *Queen Elizabeth*." His career in the RCAF took a different turn upon his return, but he was still involved in the war effort. Canadian authorities put him to good use because of his experience in the service.

I was first assigned to do propaganda and recruiting among French Canadians. I don't want to exaggerate, but I believe I was one of the first French Canadians to be decorated. I was probably the first or second non-commissioned officer to be awarded the Distinguished Flying Medal. They used me a lot to sell "Victory Bonds." I took part in those campaigns held every six months. I also went to schools to tell young men that we were at war and that it was possible to return from it. I told them to finish their schooling and to be patient, that they'd get their chance to go. I think that the fact that I had thirty-eight missions under my belt and had returned in one piece impressed them. I later became an instructor at No. 9 Bombing and Gunnery School in Mont-Joli, Quebec, and in 1944 I was posted to No. 10 Bombing and Gunnery School in Mount Pleasant, Prince Edward Island. I was chief instructor with the rank of flight lieutenant.

It was during his stint at No. 9 Bombing and Gunnery School that he was presented with his award. Air Vice-Marshal Adélard Raymond pinned the DFM on Pichette at a ceremony in Mont-Joli in April 24, 1943. The citation accompanying the medal read in part: "Flight Sergeant

Pichette has participated as an air gunner in numerous attacks over enemy and enemy occupied territory. On one occasion he took part in a daylight attack on two enemy battle-cruisers." It was at this time that Pichette married Florence Oldscamp, from Ste-Anne-de-Restigouche in Quebec. Then, in August 1945, he was demobilized.

Pichette's most precious memory of his stay in England was of the friendliness and openness of the people. "We were well received by the British. You were simply a Canadian even if you had a French accent. It wasn't the same mentality of 'goddam Frenchman' found in Canada, in places like Campbellton where I grew up. I found that fantastic. They called us 'bloody Colonials' but it was all in fun."

Roger Pichette and his wife Florence had four children. He entered provincial politics in 1952, and was the Progressive Conservative MLA for Restigouche until 1960. He was minister of industry and development in the cabinet of Hugh John Flemming. From 1960 until 1980, he was an insurance and real estate agent in Campbellton. He ran unsuccessfully in the 1979 federal election. He sat on New Brunswick's Bicentennial Commission in 1984, and was a member of the Appeals Board of Veterans Affairs from 1985 until 1989. Pichette retired in 1990 and moved to Moncton.

Chapter Three

"I was always apprehensive"
The Story of Ulysse Gallant

When war broke out in Europe in September 1939, Ulysse Gallant, a teenager from Moncton, was already serving in the non-permanent active militia. At the end of the war in 1945, he held the rank of pilot officer in the RCAF and was decorated with the Distinguished Flying Cross. He had also married a British woman, who came to Canada as his war bride.

Ulysse Gallant set aside his schoolbooks in the summer of 1939 to join the army, but his tour of service only lasted eight months. "I was in the army, with the New Brunswick Rangers, before war was declared. We guarded bridges around Gayton, near Calhoun [in the Memramcook Valley]. One day, Captain Hudson arrived and said: 'Gallant, come with me.' I asked where we were going. He replied that my father had told them that I wasn't eighteen. I left the army and went to commercial college before getting a job at Canadian National."

His return to civilian life did not stop him from thinking about military service, and as soon as he turned eighteen, he enlisted in the RCAF. "I joined on January 7, 1941. I don't know why I chose the air force instead of the army. It wasn't because I had eyes to become a pilot. I went to Toronto [No. 1 Manning Depot] before coming back to No. 8 Service Flying School in Lakeburn. I was in the materials purchase section. At the end of 1941, I crossed overseas. I was stationed at the RCAF general headquarters in London."

At the time, the British capital was the target of constant German bombing raids. "I was going back to my lodgings when an air raid began. The railroad ran in front of the house where I was staying. I ducked under a tree and could hear the warden yelling to take cover because the alarm had sounded. As soon as he turned the corner, I started to cross when I suddenly felt something whistle by my ear. It was a piece of anti-aircraft shrapnel. I burnt my fingers trying to pick it up. I grasped it with my handkerchief. I kept it for years."

Air raid warnings provided a certain diversion from life at headquarters, where things were usually monotonous even if he met famous people once in a while.

I saw "Buzz" Beurling[13] when I was at HQ in London. I was walking down a hall when I saw a guy in front of me wearing a squashed officer's hat. The squadron leader, an officer of the permanent force, came out of his office and yelled that the man was a disgrace to the air force. The guy answered that he was Flying Officer "Buzz" Beurling. If the squadron leader could have dug a hole in the floor, he would have jumped in. Beurling had just arrived from Malta.

Despite having met the greatest Canadian fighter pilot of the war, Gallant was not happy where he was. He wanted to see action.

I asked for a transfer to aircrew. They asked if I had completed high school. When I replied I hadn't, they told me I needn't bother to ask. After that, I went to night school at the London School of Economics to follow correspondence courses organized by the Canadian Legion. I stayed in London about a year before being transferred to Exeter, in Devonshire, where I opened the general headquarters of No. 2 District. When I got good grades on my courses in London, I was called for training overseas. At the time, that was Canada for us.[14] I returned to Canada [in 1943]. I remember them telling me that they didn't need pilots

---

13 George "Buzz" Beurling, from Verdun, Quebec, was a fighter pilot with the RAF and accumulated thirty-three and a third victories against the German and Italian air forces during the war. He was the hero of Malta, where he shot down twenty-seven enemy aircraft in fourteen days during the summer of 1942.

14 It was in Canada, under the aegis of the British Commonwealth Air Training Plan, that the vast majority of airmen from the Commonwealth trained between 1939 and 1945.

but machine gunners. I trained as a machine gunner in Mont-Joli, Quebec, and in London, Ontario, before going back to England. I arrived back in England in April 1944. I joined 432 Squadron. We flew Wellingtons.

Gallant's initiation in a bomber was quick in coming. At the end of his first sortie, he wondered if the next ones would be the same even if he and his crew hadn't seen the enemy.

My first sortie was a diversion raid. We left England heading for Norway and Sweden to attract German fighters. After some time, we turned around and quickly came back. The bombers of the RCAF and the RAF going out on raids could pass more easily because German fighters which had taken off to chase us had to land to refuel. I remember that first mission because the door to my turret in the rear of the Wellington didn't close properly. Wind blew in and I was freezing. I told myself that I'd never be able to endure thirty sorties like that because I'd freeze to death. After doing two or three diversion raids, we were sent to a conversion unit to train on Halifax bombers.

The Handley Page Halifax bomber, a four-engine aircraft, was larger, faster, better armed, and could climb higher than the twin-engine Vickers Wellington. For Gallant, the Halifax had another advantage one needed to be wary of: "In the Halifax, we had heated silk underwear. When we returned to England after a sortie, we had to unplug our underwear so that the cold kept us alert. If a guy stayed connected, he could fall asleep. Many were shot down because the tail gunner fell asleep."

It was in the warmth of a Halifax bomber that Gallant experienced war in the air for the first time.

My first mission in the Halifax was a night raid [on October 6, 1944]. The second and third ones were also at night. The third was against Bochum [in the Ruhr Valley]. We were criticized for

A Handley Page Halifax Mk. III bomber from No. 432 Squadron lands at
East Moor, Yorkshire, at the end of November 1944.

DND / with permission from the RCAF photo unit, PL-40488

that raid. The intelligence service should have known that the
Germans had anti-aircraft guns on rail cars. The flak was thick.
We were in the second group and could see many bombers on fire
and being shot down. Our group of planes and the others following turned sharply and didn't even come close to the target. It
would have been suicide.

Two or three sorties later, we were told we were going on
another raid against Bochum, a daylight operation. There would
only be RCAF bombers. They wanted the mission to be completed this time. It was more unnerving at night than in daytime
because at night we could see the flak bursts, the cones of light
from the projectors in the clouds, and the glare of exploding aircraft. During the day, we could see if another bomber was above

us and opening its bomb bay doors, ready to drop its load. We told the pilot to turn to port. We saw the bombs falling next to us. At night, we couldn't see anything. We did 60 percent of our sorties at night and 40 percent during the day.

It wasn't funny at night. When we began our raids, the Germans sent up their fighters to find us. German controllers on the ground told them in which direction we were heading. Throughout the war, both sides tried to find inventions to get an edge. The Germans had their radar. We had "window," which we dropped to jam their radar. It was quite sophisticated near the end. Nothing happened on only about ten of the thirty-two missions I went on.

Things got dangerous when the squadron was sent on raids against the Ruhr Valley.

One evening while approaching Gelsenkirchen [northeast of Essen], the navigator told us he had just seen a German fighter under our wing. I had seen him three or four minutes before. I didn't want to worry the crew because the fighter was beneath us and couldn't bring his machine guns to bear on us. The navigator, who had only small-calibre machine guns in the nose, told us he was going to shoot down the German. I told him to do nothing. The task of the tail gunner was to protect the aircraft at all times, especially when nearing the target. We shouldn't open fire when over the target because there was a risk of hitting other bombers. It wasn't worth firing on the German fighter if he wasn't bothering us. If we shot at him, he could come after us. If I had told the pilot to "corkscrew starboard," I would have had him in my sights. I couldn't have missed my shot. Our goal wasn't to shoot down enemy planes but to drop our bombs and return to England. I still remember that I could see the German pilot's face. His fighter was under the wing, not more than 200 yards away. He was looking at us and I was looking at him. We dropped our bombs and turned for home. I'm telling you I was watching to see if he followed!

German anti-aircraft defences were not limited to fighters, which had a hard time finding the Halifax bombers in the dark. Even if their radar system guided them to the bombers, the pilots needed to see the aircraft before attacking. Powerful projectors on the ground lit up the skies. For a bomber crew, being caught by them was a terrifying experience when flying at 12,000 or 15,000 feet. "The Germans had fortified the defences around Cologne. We were on a night operation when caught in the light cone as we left Cologne. We stayed in that light for at least three minutes. In a case like that, the tail gunner told the pilot to veer left or right to escape. When the aircraft was out of the light, we still had to be on our guard because the fighters had probably seen where we were."

Gallant remembered that these searchlights sometimes helped bomber crews. "Another time, while leaving Düsseldorf or Dortmund after dropping our bombs, I saw something fly by on the right of our plane. I didn't know if it was one of our bombers or what because it was so dark. A cone lit up the object and I saw that the plane had only one engine. The fighter turned and I gave him three or four bursts from my machine guns. It disappeared. Upon arrival at base, I claimed a 'probable'."

After the Allied invasion of Normandy on June 6, 1944, the life expectancy of bomber crews increased dramatically. The Allies dominated the skies over western Europe and Germany. The German air force was short of pilots and fuel for its fighters. And the thousands of bomber raids finally bore fruit by reducing Germany's capacity to produce the weapons needed to pursue hostilities. The *Luftwaffe* refused to engage in daylight combat against American bombers, which were now protected by long-range fighters. At night, however, the situation was different because RCAF and RAF bombers didn't benefit from fighter protection.

Gallant and his crew completed many sorties without incident, but on the return from a raid against Essen in the winter of 1945, their aircraft was badly damaged by an enemy fighter.

We thought we had been hit by a diving fighter. There was a hole behind my head and the controls to the rudder had been cut. The aircraft began to fall and everything was shaking like hell. The pilot told us to get ready to bail out. I went over the whole drill, all I had learned during training. I made sure my parachute was well fastened. I turned my turret, lowered my guns, put a foot outside and unhooked the heating. I did all I had to do before jumping. I had my hand on the oxygen feed, ready to unplug it. I waited and waited for the pilot to tell us to jump. I told myself that something was terribly wrong. I had unplugged my intercom. I plugged it in and heard the captain yell to the flight engineer to go check in back because I might be wounded. I immediately answered the captain that I was okay. The navigator told the pilot that we were no longer losing altitude and that it would be better to jump over France. All of the crew agreed. When we reached France, the navigator informed the pilot that we could reach England because we were maintaining our altitude. The wings started to ice up when we began crossing the English Channel. We were lower than we should have been. We finally saw the coast and made a crash landing in a field on the south coast of England. Nobody was injured.

The first to come to our aid drove an American Jeep. He asked if anyone was hurt and then took off. An RAF truck arrived shortly after and took us to a nearby RAF base. The chaplain was there when we arrived. He gave us a glass of rum when we went in to report. We drank the rum before speaking. The intelligence officer said: "You seem exhausted. You can go sleep in the hangar." We were all asleep within two minutes after hitting the beds. We had spent six hours in the air and hadn't eaten for at least eight hours. The next morning, one of our bombers, which had landed at that base for repairs, was ready to return to 432 Squadron. We hopped aboard. The plane's hydraulic system failed when we arrived at East Moor. We didn't have any brakes. The pilot tried to land in a field but he hit barbed wire. We somehow managed

Unidentified crew from No. 432 Squadron getting ready to leave on a bombing sortie.
LAC/ PA-142229

to land. When we got to our barracks, our personal effects were gone. We had been reported missing. In less than twenty-four hours, we had crashed once and come close to crashing a second time.

Gallant and his crew were luckier than some from their own squadron or other air force friends. Some had a feeling that their time was running out.

There were two guys from another crew, a mid-gunner and a tail gunner, who liked to play tricks on us all the time. They were full of life. They were always the first in our changing room where we put on our flight suits. They would tie knots in our silk long johns and played other tricks like that. Both of them were very quiet at briefing one evening. Many of us noticed this. We never heard from them again; they were shot down that night.

I also remember Jimmy Small from Moncton. He served with another squadron not far from East Moor. Another guy, Ivan Terry, and I had a forty-eight-hour pass and went to see him. We chatted while drinking beer in a pub but Jimmy wasn't very talkative. We told him it would be his turn to visit us next time at East Moor. He said he thought he could come down the next weekend. We made arrangements. While returning to base, Ivan told me that something wasn't right with Jimmy, that he must have a cold or something. That evening, Jimmy was shot down. He was taken prisoner. I saw Jimmy after the war and he told me his story. He was picked up by a girl shortly after he hit the ground. She told him she was taking him to some people who could help him escape. She must have been a spy because she called the Germans. They put him in the back seat of a car and started questioning him, a revolver pointed at his face. He gave his name and number. They told him they knew his squadron was in Yorkshire because another captured crew had given them information they wanted to confirm. Even with a revolver between both eyes, Jimmy said nothing.

No. 432 Squadron had been in East Moor since mid-September 1943. Living conditions were quite good, but they were a lot better at American bases, where Gallant and his crew landed occasionally. "The base at East Moor was on a large farm. We parked our bombers behind a barn or under trees. We dispersed them all over the place. It wasn't that bad at East Moor. The food was good. If we were running low on fuel returning from a raid or if our base was iced in, we loved landing at an American base when possible. There was ice cream, eggs, bacon, and real orange juice. The Americans even brought ice cream on raids and ate it on their way back."

Food was not the only difference between the American and Canadian air forces, and the Canadians wouldn't have changed places with American flyers. They had different approaches to bombing: Americans flew in tight formations and bombed only in daytime, while Canadians and British favoured night raids and looser formations. Gallant felt that this fundamental difference led to the loss of many American crews.

I was on an American base once when their planes started coming in. They had been hit hard by the enemy. They were taking men out on stretchers. When they flew, they didn't break formation because they only had two or three navigators which they had to follow. They couldn't fly at night because they got lost. We had a navigator in every bomber. We were quite independent. Sometimes we didn't see anyone around even in daylight. The American bombers, the B-17s, had more armaments than ours. There was a gunner on each side, one in the tail, and one on top. I'm sure some of them shot down their own Flying Fortresses because their formations we so tight.

In the spring of 1945, the war in Europe was coming to an end. Germany, crushed by bombs and Allied attacks on all sides, called upon weapons that scientists had been working on since the start of hostilities. It was during a night raid against Hamburg in April that Gallant glimpsed a strange phenomenon in the sky. He had no idea what it was.

The night of our second to last sortie, I told the pilot that I had seen an explosion on my left, at eight o'clock. The navigator recorded this. I didn't know if a plane had been hit by flak or what. A short time later, I saw a light flashing by like the devil. I had never seen anything like it before. I told the pilot. When we got to debriefing, they said I had seen a jet. I said: "What's a jet?" If the Germans had used those planes long before, I wonder what would have happened?[15]

Every time Gallant climbed into the rear turret of his Halifax bomber, he was conscious of the danger that awaited at every turn, but he mastered his fear. "There was no sortie where I wasn't afraid. I didn't shake from fear, but I was apprehensive all the time. The average life expectancy for a tail gunner was probably twelve missions."

It is easy to imagine the bonds of friendship between a small group of men who risked their lives every time duty called. This team spirit is seen

---

15   The Messerschmitt Me 262 was the first jet-propelled fighter of the Second World War. The Germans used it in the last months of the war. It reached a speed of 900 km/h and could climb higher than any other aircraft at the time. However, their number was too small to have a significant impact on the air war.

in war movies: the guys are always having a drink in a pub after a raid. Not all crews, however, conformed to this stereotype.

In our crew, we were always all Lone Rangers. The pilot and I went on leave to Scotland once. The radio operator went his way and the bombardier was married with a child. We all attended the wedding of our engineer, an Englishman. The navigator was more of an intellectual type who visited museums and things like that. The mid-gunner was an American. We seldom went out together even if we were close in the air. To complete thirty-two sorties, we had to work together and respect one another. We had to be professionals. We weren't close.

Gallant, like all Canadian aviators, was proud to wear the blue uniform of the RCAF. The wings on his tunic did not go unnoticed by women when he strolled down the street or went to dances or movies. It was while posted at RCAF headquarters in London in 1942 that he met a young woman, Joan Mitchell, who would become his wife in January 1945.

I met a woman at a dance at Hammersmith Palace. She lived in Islington. At the time, I was attending university at night, but we went on dates when I had no classes. I was then transferred back to Canada. When I returned to England, I rejoined my fiancée and we got married. One day I told Joan I wanted to visit the woman who had billeted me while I was in London at the beginning. When we got there, nothing was left. Fourteen three-storey houses in a row had been bombed. If I hadn't been transferred to aircrew, I might have stayed there, under the rubble.

Joan had lived through the German blitz on London. She was undoubtedly worried whenever her husband left on a sortie against Germany. Hundreds of young British women had married Canadian

Devastated buildings in Temple, London after a German
air raid on May 10, 1941. Alamy/ HT2075

airmen, and many of them became widows after raids against enemy
territory.

Gallant's experiences on the ground under German bombs in London
in 1941 and 1942 go a long way toward explaining his attitude as a crew
member of a Canadian bomber. "When we returned from dropping our
bombs on a city, I often thought about the people we had bombed. I also
thought of the times I was in London when the Germans bombed. It
was very bad in 1941. There was so much propaganda which said the
Germans bombed cathedrals, such as Coventry, and foster homes. After a
while, you stopped thinking about such things to keep your sanity."

No. 432 Squadron flew its last sortie on April 25, 1945. Two weeks
later, on May 8, the Allies celebrated the end of the war in Europe. The
next day, Gallant was promoted to flying officer. He was happy that the
war was over, but after thirty-two missions he volunteered to fight against
Japan. "I told the guys in the crew that by volunteering for Japan we
would be back in Canada before the others. They didn't want to. They'd

had enough. Four weeks later, I was in Dartmouth, Nova Scotia. It took the others at least another month to come back."

Gallant was already in Canada when he learned he would be receiving the DFC. The recommendation for the honour notes that the tail gunner probably saved his crew on two occasions when his bomber was attacked by German fighters.[16] The citation for the medal, which Gallant received on July 5, 1945, reads that it was given for his "courage and devotion to duty."

Ulysse and Joan had eight children. He attended Mount Allison University in Sackville, New Brunswick, and Dalhousie University in Halifax, where he obtained a Bachelor of Commerce degree. He spent a total of forty-two years with Canadian National, mostly in human resources. He became director of employment services in Moncton in 1955. Transferred to Montreal in 1960, he became the assistant to the president of CN Express. He retired in 1980, but continued working as a consultant with different government departments and agencies until 1985. The couple lived in the Shediac Bridge area.

---

16   Information on Ulysse Gallant is available online at rcafassociation.ca/heritage/search-awards.

Laurie Cormier (right) in July 1945 after his return from POW camps in Germany, with his brothers Norman (centre), who served in the navy, and André "Drake" (left), who was in the army. His brothers Léo and Joseph also served in the army during the war.

Chapter Four

The Fourteenth Mission
The Story of Joseph Laurie Cormier

The number thirteen instils fear in most superstitious people. Allied airmen who took part in raids against targets in Europe in 1943 also dreaded this number and with good cause. At that period of the Second World War, the German air force was still a considerable threat to bombers venturing over Germany and occupied countries. The life expectancy of a bomber crew was thirteen missions. Laurie Cormier, a young Acadian from Moncton, was a tail gunner on a Halifax bomber from No. 427 "Lion" Squadron of the RCAF. He returned safely from his thirteenth sortie in mid-December 1943, but his luck soon ran out: a few days later, he was shot down and became a prisoner of war.

The war gave Cormier the chance to fulfil a lifelong ambition. "I had dreamt of being involved in aviation since I was a boy. One of my heroes was Charles Lindbergh. After finishing school, I worked for a few months. I tried to join the air force in December 1941, but they told me to wait after New Year's. I enlisted in January 1942." Cormier was nineteen years old when his dream of becoming a pilot seemed about to come true when he completed his training at the base in Victoriaville, Quebec.

That's where they decided which job you would train for. I was lucky and was chosen to become a pilot. That's what I wanted.

From there, I went to Cap-de-la-Madeleine. We were forty-five student pilots. I was the third to fly solo in a Fleet Finch. I was doing well. After my first solo flight, I thought I owned the skies. One day, I was caught flying over the shipyard building corvettes in Sorel. I had flown too low and they hadn't liked that. I was warned not to do that again. I had so much confidence in myself that I wasn't paying attention to what the instructor was saying. He told me to do such and such a manoeuvre but I did something else. When the time came for me to pass the test, I didn't know how to perform the manoeuvres. I failed the exam.

Cormier's vision of obtaining his pilot's wings evaporated because of his overconfidence, but he still wanted to be an aviator. "They trained me as an air gunner in Mont-Joli, Quebec." His months of training completed, Cormier went overseas on the ocean liner *Queen Elizabeth* in April 1943. He didn't have to wait long before going out on his first sortie. "When I got to England, they sent me to Stratford-on-Avon to train on Wellington bombers. It was an OTU, an Operational Training Unit. That's where we formed crews: a pilot, a bombardier, a navigator, a radio operator, and a gunner." His first sortie, however, was not with his new crew.

The guy in charge of machine guns came from Belgium. He spoke French. One day he told me that they needed three aircraft from OTU to search the North Sea for an American bomber missing on returning from a raid against Hamburg. They usually took instructors to go on those searches, but there were not enough for three crews. I asked the Belgian if I could go. He answered that I hadn't finished my training yet. I said that it didn't matter. He asked permission from the commanding officer, and that's how I went on my first sortie. They put me in the forward turret. It was an international crew: the pilot was British, the navigator was from Australia, the radio operator was an American serving in the RCAF, I was in front, and the Belgian was in the rear turret. We did what we called a "square search."

Their training completed, Cormier and the other crew members were given a week's leave. Before leaving they were told that, on their return, they would join No. 425 "Alouette" Squadron, which had just left for North Africa. But when they got back, they were assigned to 427 "Lion" Squadron in Yorkshire.

We arrived at Leeming at the end of June. When we got there, we picked up another gunner, the mid-upper, a Barnes from Ottawa. He was older than the others, who were all between twenty and twenty-two years old. Our pilot was Rudy Lacerte, a francophone from Saskatchewan. The others were St-Pierre, Little, Kiteley, and Wilkins. I think our first raid took us to Ludwigshafen. Everything went well. All our raids, except one, were against Germany. One time we dropped our bombs in the Calais area, where they believed there were ammunition dumps in the woods.

In mid-December 1943, the crew of Halifax bomber ZL976 K left on their thirteenth sortie. The men were apprehensive because they were undertaking that mission where the odds of survival turned against them.

It's funny; it's a thing I couldn't understand, that fear we had all the time. I loved flying in spite of that. I wasn't any more afraid than the others. We had problems during that thirteenth sortie. The canopy above the pilot blew off and air was rushing in. We turned around and dropped our large bomb in the North Sea on our way back to base. We got a lecture from the commanding officer. Turnbull [Wing Commander R.S. Turnbull] didn't want any "turnarounds" as he called them. He told us it would be the last time we returned without dropping our bombs on the target. We had completed our thirteenth mission without being hit.

Cormier and his crew were safe and sound. They probably breathed a bit easier. They were now veterans—they had beaten the odds.

On December 20, we went out on our fourteenth sortie. It was a raid against Frankfurt-am-Main. I had fallen ill, I had a cold. The doctor told me I couldn't fly for a week. That evening, I went to briefing with the others even if I had a replacement. I introduced him to the crew. The pilot, Lacerte, told me he didn't like the idea of flying with someone he didn't know. He asked if I wanted to go with them. I explained that the doctor had said I shouldn't fly but that I'd go if he wanted.

The rest of Cormier's story would have been very different if he had followed the squadron doctor's advice.

I had forgotten the key to my locker. We were in a hurry to leave, and I said I needed to get my key to get my flying suit from my locker. An American who worked with the gunnery officer was present. He told me I didn't have time to go and that I could use his things. He asked me to return them the next morning. He had a nice leather flying suit. Our Halifax bomber was old. The squadron commander came to see us at dispersal before we left and told us it was our last sortie with this aircraft. Tomorrow, we'd be getting a new Halifax with radial engines. Everything started to go wrong as soon as we gained altitude. I was starved of oxygen in the rear turret. I had a hard time breathing. When I told the engineer, he turned up the flow. As we got over the English Channel, the engineer began complaining that one of the engines wasn't running right, that its speed kept changing. We didn't know what to do because he couldn't fix the problem. We finally decided to head back to base. After changing direction, we told ourselves that we couldn't go back. We remembered what Turnbull, the squadron commander, had said last time. We headed back for Germany. When we did this, we lost time and were lower than we should have been. We trailed behind the rest of the squadron.

Had the crew of Halifax ZL976 K been able to imagine the fate that awaited them, they surely would have preferred facing the wrath of Wing Commander Turnbull and returned to Leeming.

The German fighters, the Messerschmitt 110s, had a type of radar, the *Lichtenstein*, which allowed them to see us at night. In the back of our bomber, we had a monitor which went "beep-beep" when one of those enemy planes got behind us. The monitor didn't work well and we had turned it off. We didn't know the enemy was behind us. We were hit and one of our engines caught fire. My turret had been hit and I could no longer shoot. I remember seeing something like a flash. Once we were on fire, he came back after us. I could see him. He fired, and I could see tracer from his cannons which looked like golf balls. I thought he was going to cut our plane in half. I could see the bullets from Barnes's machine guns zoom over my head. I was telling the pilot to dive, to climb, to go left or right when the enemy attacked. I could clearly see him when he fired. All of sudden, he left us alone. I don't know if Barnes hit him or not.

I thought he had hit us again about twenty times, but after he was gone, we realized we hadn't been hit again. We were attacked twenty minutes before getting to Frankfurt. It must have been around eight o'clock at night. The pilot shut down the damaged engine and opened the fire extinguishers. That didn't work, because the fire was in an oil reservoir behind the engine, near one of the wheels of the landing gear. After dropping our bombs on target, we turned to go back to England. We flew for about twenty-five minutes before the fire really took hold. Pieces of the aircraft began breaking off. The pilot told us it was time to bail out. We were trying to make it to France. We had trouble getting Wilkins, the Englishman, to jump. He sat in the emergency exit and was frozen there. Someone had to push him out. The pilot usually had a dorsal parachute on the back of his seat but that night he had a frontal one. I had the parachute and wanted to make sure he put it on. I was standing next to him while the others jumped. He said: "Get the hell out of here!" That's when I bailed out. It was dark and I couldn't see the ground when I jumped. I saw it just before I landed. We all jumped one after the other but we didn't meet up once on the ground. It wasn't like in the movies, where the guys find each other after bailing out. I landed somewhere in western Germany [possibly near Trier].

It was December 20, 1943, five days before Christmas, and Cormier found himself somewhere in enemy territory in the dead of night. He had no idea where he was, he didn't know the terrain, had nothing to eat, and was unarmed. His adventure was only beginning.

I walked for four nights. I stayed in the woods during the day and walked at night towards France. One night I was walking in a field when I saw a mound of dirt. I dug in it and found some potatoes. That's where the Germans stored them for winter. I ate a few. By the fourth day, December 24, I was really tired because I hadn't slept since I bailed out. I hadn't walked very far. I lay down under a tree. I was sleeping when I heard bells around noon. I told myself they must be church bells. All of a sudden, two young men, members of the Hitler Youth, appeared. One woke me up and the other ran to the nearby village. He really surprised me because he spoke English. He asked: "English?" I replied: "No, Canadian." He asked where I was going. I told him I was returning to England. He said he didn't think that would be the case because guys like me became prisoners. I had cut my flying boots because I had trouble walking in them. I couldn't have run with them on my feet. I was too tired to try to escape.

The young man told me to follow him to the village. We arrived at his house. He went to speak with his mother at the back door. He asked if I was hungry. I answered that I was. His mother was ready to go in to get me something when two soldiers arrived with the other young man. When she saw this, she did nothing because she was probably afraid of having problems if she gave me food. The two soldiers took me to city hall. They sat me down. All of a sudden, an older man entered. He walked with a cane. He was probably a soldier who had been wounded. He started yelling and tried to hit me with his cane. I lifted my arm to stop him from hitting me in the face. One of the soldiers got mad and put him out. From the village, I was taken to a small camp for officers, an *Oflag* [*Offizierlager*]. We stayed outside by the entrance. That's where I saw my pilot Rudy Lacerte, but they stopped us from talking to each other.

Cormier spent only a few hours at this camp before being sent to another camp, where he began to understand that he was now a prisoner of war and that his days as a crew member of a Canadian bomber were over and done with. Like all Allied airmen, he had precise instructions on what he could say if captured by the enemy.

That night [Christmas Eve], they took us by truck to Frankfurt, where the interrogation camp was located. I don't know why, but we went to the train station. I saw the damage we had done. The roof was caved in. The Royal Air Force was out that evening and the sirens began to wail. Everyone went down to the shelters below. They took us too and sat us on the ground. People walked by and spat on us. Women were furious. Our two guards saw to it that the civilians didn't cause us any harm. The RAF didn't bomb Frankfurt but must have bombed elsewhere. From the station, we took a small streetcar to go to the *Dulag Luft*.[17]
  When I arrived at interrogation, a German made me get undressed. He took my flight jacket, the one I had borrowed

---

17 *Dulag Luft*, short for *Durchgangslager der Luftwaffe*, was a transit camp run by the German air force.

from the American, and threw it in a corner. I told him I wanted it back. He replied that it didn't belong to me but to them. He showed me the label inside which said "Air Ministry" and said that what belonged to the Air Ministry was now theirs. They then locked me up in a cell heated by radiators under the window. The cell was very small. There was a little bed and just enough room to pace around. It was hot but I couldn't open the window. After some time, I got it open. A guard came in later in the evening and started scolding me because I had opened the window. I said: "Too hot, too hot." He went out and came back about fifteen minutes later. He took me to another cell, one under construction. In that one, there was no window and no heat. I froze all night.

Meanwhile, in Léger Corner [now Dieppe], New Brunswick, Sergeant Cormier's mother learned by telegram on December 23 that her son was "reported missing after air operations overseas on December 21."[18] A few days later, a letter arrived from the commanding officer of 427 Squadron, Wing Commander Turnbull, written on December 21, the day after Cormier went missing. Turnbull's words were comforting: "Joseph[19] had only recently become a member of this Squadron's personnel, but during the short length of time that he was with us, his ability and cheerful personality marked him as one of our most promising Operational Crew members."[20] He reminded Mrs. Cormier that there was a possibility her son was a prisoner of war.

Back in Germany, Cormier was being held in what was more than a simple POW camp. The *Dulag Luft* in Oberursel, just outside Frankfurt, was the main interrogation centre for Allied airmen shot down over Germany. It was run by officers who had become masters of interrogation techniques. Cormier would always remember Christmas Day, 1943.

18 Telegram from the RCAF Casualties Officer to Mrs. André Cormier, December 23, 1943.
19 In the RCAF, the first name appearing on the birth certificate was usually used, thus Joseph.
20 Letter from Wing Commander Turnbull to Mrs. André Cormier, December 21, 1943, received in January 1944. Mrs. Cormier officially learned on January 22 that her son was a prisoner of war.

On Christmas night, a German wearing an air force uniform came in and gave me a form he said was from the Red Cross. It asked for your name, your rank, and other questions we had been warned not to answer. I put down my name and my rank. I signed. The German looked at the sheet and said: "You didn't put down anything!" I answered that I wasn't supposed to answer those questions. He said that I was probably a spy if I didn't know the answers. I said: "I'm not a spy, I have dog tags." He replied that it was easy to have those pieces of identity and that they got rid of spies, executed them at dawn. I was so tired that I told myself that they were the ones running things and that they could do what they wanted with me.

An hour or two later, two guards armed with rifles came to get me. It was early Christmas morning. I thought they were going to put me against a wall to execute me. We came out of the prison, crossed a large parade square, and entered a building with offices. That's where I met the interrogation officer. He offered me a cigarette as soon as I sat down. I told him I didn't smoke. He started asking me questions, but I didn't answer even if I knew many of the answers. He wanted to know our aircraft number but I didn't know it. Even if I had wanted to tell him, I would have been unable. I saw that number every day but it never registered. On his desk he had a large book with the number 427 on it. I saw it but it didn't ring a bell. The German officer wanted me to give him the name of the gunnery leader because he knew I was a gunner. In a corner of his office, there was a "Gee Box," a machine to aid navigation. He asked if I knew what it was. I answered that I was a gunner and didn't know anything about that. Before ending the interrogation, he took the large book and began answering some of the questions he had asked. The book was full of newspaper clippings. He told me I had crossed from New York on the *Queen Elizabeth* and a lot of other things. He asked if I knew that Flight Lieutenant Laird had been awarded the Distinguished Flying Cross. It was only later in the POW camp that I learned from another 427 crew that Laird had won it. The questioning took place on Christmas Day. I hadn't had my Christmas turkey. I was then sent to join the other prisoners.

Once the interrogations were over at the *Dulag Luft* transit camp, the men were sent to regular POW camps. After eight days, Cormier left for *Stalag* IVb at Mühlberg, in eastern Germany. The trip covered some 350 kilometres.

It took us two days to get there. We climbed aboard freight cars marked 40 men / 8 horses. We didn't know where we were going. The train stopped somewhere in a large marshalling yard. That night, the air force bombed the station and the cars were bouncing on the rails. We were lucky not to be hit. The train got to Mühlberg in the evening. It was cold and rainy. We walked from the station to the camp. When I saw the camp, I told myself that I'd never get out. It was a camp for soldiers. The Germans told us we'd be sent to an air force camp later. We were five from our crew. I think the others were sent to *Stalag Luft* III at Sagan.

The *Stalag* in Mühlberg housed mainly soldiers, but there was also a small number of airmen. The Germans did not keep their promise to transfer Cormier to an air force camp, and the young Acadian spent the last sixteen months of the war in Mülhberg.

There were between 10,000 and 12,000 men in the camp, which was divided in compounds. There was one compound for the Royal Air Force, one for the French, one for the Russians, one for the Poles, and one for English soldiers. Three members of our crew were sent to a barracks with Englishmen from the 8th Army who had been captured in North Africa. The other two were sent to another section. We were about one hundred per barrack. In ours, there were three-tiered bunks. The toilets made of cement were in the middle of the building and at each end were the sleep-

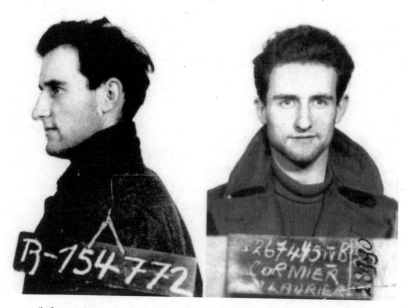

(left to right) Laurie Cormier, photo probably taken at the *Dulag Luft* shortly after his capture—it includes his RCAF service number (R-154772); Cormier's identity card photo and POW number (267445) at *Stalag* IVb, Mühlberg. Collection of Laurie Cormier

ing quarters. We didn't have any water to wash up. From time to time, we went for a shower in another building, a community shower. During the day we could use the latrines in a brick building. It had twenty-four seats.

Conditions in the camp were not that bad when I arrived. What I found hardest was not having enough to eat. The non-commissioned officers didn't have to work. I would have loved to work. I would have gone to work on farms to get more to eat. At the beginning, we received Red Cross parcels on a regular basis. Sometimes, we had to share one between two guys. As soon as the invasion [of Normandy] began, the parcels were less frequent and we had to share one between four or five guys. There were good things in them. The ones from Canada were the favourites.

The Americans and the British also sent some, but it was the Canadian one which was the best. Even Canadian cigarettes were worth more than American ones. Near the end we weren't getting Red Cross parcels. We only had German rations. When they gave us pea soup, one had to search for a long time before finding the peas.

Cormier's imprisonment took on a dimension that differed from the lives of airmen of lower rank, who were forced to work. Boredom and the lack of activities were a major problem for prisoners who had nothing to do but twiddle their thumbs most of the time.

We got up early in the morning. We walked around the camp a lot. We spent a lot of time doing nothing. From time to time, I'd sit with someone to have a chat. We often played cards in the evening and there was entertainment sometimes. There was always someone who could play the accordion or some other instrument. We had volleyball teams in summer. I was a member of the second British team. Our team was quite good. There was nothing much to do besides that. I often told myself that I'd be better off in the Royal Air Force compound. The guys caused trouble all the time. After a while, I understood that I was better where I was, with the soldiers. I got along very well with them. They told stories of their time in North Africa. There was a small building in the RAF compound which served as a library, but there were no books. The prisoners began digging a tunnel from it. They were beyond the barbed wire and were in a wheat field. When they were about to try to get out, a German ran over it with a tractor. One of the wheels collapsed the tunnel.

In order to while away the long hours of inactivity, the prisoners harassed their guards in various ways. For many of them, it became a game that broke the monotony of life behind barbed wire.

Some of the POW camps in Germany and the occupied countries.
Mühlberg, Lamsdorf, and Moosburg were mainly for captured soldiers.
The *Dulag Luft* was an interrogation centre for downed Allied airmen.

Ronald Cormier / Mike Bechthold

When a German entered our barrack, the first guy who saw him yelled Bugs Bunny to warn us. When the guards counted us during *Appell*, we counted along with them and they lost their count. There was one guard, a tall lanky fellow; we called him *Hopalong Cassidy* because he bounced when he walked. One day, I was in the front row and began counting with him. When he got to me, he was all flustered. He had to start all over. I thought he had forgotten what I had done. When he got back to me, he took out his revolver, his Luger, and pointed it right at my nose. He started saying what he was going to do to me. Even if I didn't understand, I never tried to confuse him after that. Sometimes, guys changed places to be counted twice. The more often we did that, the longer we spent on *Appell*.

Relations between prisoners and their warders were not always adversarial. Connections developed between the two groups, and Cormier was not the only one to benefit from this black market.

Cigarettes were money in the camps. My godfather sold cigarettes in Canada. I wrote a small note and asked him to send me as many as he could. He knew I didn't smoke but I didn't tell him they were like money. I often traded them for bread with the German guards. Other guys exchanged them for parts to build small radios. The Germans searched long and wide for those radios. They nearly destroyed the barracks but never found them. I never knew where they were hidden and I wasn't interested in knowing where they were. All I wanted was to have news from the BBC every night. A man listened in secret, wrote it down on a small note which passed from one barrack to another. We gathered quietly to hear a guy reading the news. The next day, we told the Germans what had happened the day before. They told us it wasn't true but a week later they'd come and tell us it was. From time to time, the Germans infiltrated SS soldiers dressed in British uniforms and speaking perfect English to gather information. We were warned to be careful. When someone you didn't know sat next to you, you got up and left. When we found a spy, he was escorted to the gate.

The long months of captivity were not conducive to sustaining the morale of men trained to fight. Even though they got news from clandestine radios and played cat and mouse with their guards, they needed tangible signs that the war was continuing and the Allies had the upper hand.

After the invasion of France, it was impressive to see up to a thousand bombers, Flying Fortresses, escorted by fighters, Mustangs, fly over nearly every day. We could hear them approach nearly half an hour before we saw them. Once the bombers had dropped their loads, the fighters had nothing to do. Since the Germans didn't want to go up to fight, the American fighters descended to get them. It was good for morale. One day, two Mustangs which were chasing a German fighter, a Focke-Wulf 190, flew over the camp at ground level. Bullets from their machine guns hit the camp as they flew by. They shot down the fighter a bit further on. One man was shaving near a window. A bullet hit his razor and took the skin off two of his fingers. He never found his razor. He was lucky the bullet had passed a few inches from his face.

Not all the incidents Cormier witnessed in camp ended on such a happy note. A German airfield was located nearby, and some pilots buzzed the camp to scare the prisoners. On April 30, 1944, he witnessed a tragic ending.

I remember a guy [Sergeant Herbert Mallory] from Plaster Rock who was killed while walking with another man. It was shortly before the end of the war. It was around seven in the evening. I was playing volleyball a bit farther on. A German plane, a JU-88, was buzzing the camp. All of a sudden, the pilot flew too low behind two men who were walking and when he pulled up, the tail wheel of the plane hit the Canadian in the back of the head. The guy from Plaster Rock was killed and the other man injured.[21] The JU-88 went through a barbed wire fence and over us. We were sure he was going to crash but he kept going. We later

---

21 This incident is also related by Dave MacIntosh in "Fill in the Gaps," *Legion Magazine* (June 1985).

learned that they had found the pilot and that he was supposed to be court-martialled.

In Mühlberg, as in other German camps, authorities and guards usually respected the rules governing the treatment of prisoners, but it didn't happen without the detainees seeing to it.

In our camp, there was a guy we called the man of confidence, "Snowshoe" Myers. He intervened with the Germans on our behalf. There was a small Jewish fellow named Carl with him. Carl was born in Berlin and fled Germany in time. When he got to England, he joined the army and was sent to the 8th Army in North Africa, where he was captured. He spoke German well. As a small Jew, he wasn't afraid of the Germans because he knew he was protected. When "Snowshoe" went to see the Germans, Carl was his interpreter.

Despite their dealings with the camp authorities, the prisoners rubbed shoulders with guards who did not always see things the same way as their superiors. The guards' attitudes were often influenced by events outside the camp.

Most of the guards were veterans of the First World War. I remember that a guard sergeant's whole family was killed during the bombing of Dresden[22] by the Royal Air Force and the Americans near the end of the war. The next morning, he had us come out for *Appell* at seven in the morning. We stood there until noon. Some of the men became weak and others fell down.

One of the guards was younger than the others. We called him "Blondie." He had been wounded on the Russian front. He was cruel towards the Russian prisoners. He often beat them with a belt. He was less cruel with us because he respected us more.

---

22   Dresden was bombed on February 13 and 14, 1945, causing about 25,000 casualties.

During the winter of 1945, Nazi Germany, attacked in the west by the Canadians, British, and Americans and in the east by the Russians, was slowly falling apart even if its military power remained considerable. Its industries and railways were the targets of unrelenting bombing by Allied air forces. The destruction of the means of transportation had repercussions not only on Germans but also on POWs. As Cormier relates, "It was cold in the barracks at night in winter. I didn't get undressed to go to bed. It was the only way to keep warm. There was no straw left in our mattresses and we only had a small blanket. There was no heat at all at night. The Germans gave us only enough coal to keep the stove going during the day. I fell ill during the winter of '44-45. I was coughing; I thought my lungs were going to burst. I went to what we called the *Lazarett*, the hospital, but they couldn't do anything because they had no medication. I got better by myself after a while. It was really hard."

The spring of 1945 brought not only milder weather but the liberation of millions of prisoners of war by the Russians in eastern Germany. On the morning of April 22, Cormier and the other POWs in Mühlberg got up to go to *Appell* as usual.

We saw there were no guards in the towers. We walked to the main gate, which was wide open. There were no guards there either. The Germans had flown the coop during the night. Before the Russians arrived at our camp, our officers gave us the choice of crossing the Elbe River on barges to head towards the Americans. We didn't want to. Others—Poles, I believe—left. The Americans didn't know who they were and attacked them. Some were killed. Around noon we saw the first Russians going by on horseback. They were Cossacks. A small reconnaissance aircraft landed near the camp shortly after. The pilot came out. He was as drunk as a skunk. He came to see us and climbed back in his plane. We told ourselves that he was too drunk to take off, but, no, he left in a cloud of dust. Other Russians arrived later. There were even women with big rifles slung over their shoulders directing traffic. Russian soldiers warned us not to touch their women. We left camp in search of food. We went to a farm where we caught a small pig. We killed it, cooked it, and ate it right away. We were all sick later.

Even if the German guards had left and the camp's gates were wide open, that did not mean the prisoners were free to go as they pleased. Quite the contrary, they became pawns in a political chess game between the Western Allies and the Soviet Union.

We were about fifty miles from the American lines. Some guys who had been captured after the invasion were still in quite good shape. Men from the Winnipeg Rifles tried to reach the Americans, but the Russians caught them and brought them back to camp. One day, the Russians entered the camp with doctors who told us the water was bad and that we had to march about twenty miles to Reisa [south of Mühlberg], where there was a German camp with brick barracks. We stayed there for a while. I remember the day the war ended. The Russians were fishing in the Elbe with grenades. When they exploded, the fish rose to the surface, belly up. Reisa was on the other side of the Elbe. The Americans came to get us. We walked up to a field and had to wait for the Americans to bring the Russians who had been captured in France and elsewhere. It was a sort of exchange.

Once the deal was sealed between the Americans and Russians, Cormier finally found his long-awaited freedom.

We boarded trucks driven by Black soldiers, trucks of the Red Ball Express. We got on the Autobahn to Halle, where we waited for a week or two for the Americans to fly us out with DC-3s to Belgium. We stayed in a sort of convent. I fell ill but I don't remember what I had. The RAF finally came to get us. We were flown to England where I spent a week in hospital. I think I was sick because I had eaten too much while in Halle. I had lost forty pounds. I didn't weigh more than 100 pounds. It didn't take me long to gain weight once I was in England.

Cormier arrived in England on May 27. A week later, he sent a telegram to his mother to let her know he was in good health. After leaving hospital, he did not return to 427 Squadron. He had been a warrant officer for two and a half years, but after having suffered the ordeal of a POW for more than sixteen months, he felt insulted by the RCAF.

When we got to Bournemouth, they interviewed us to get our commissions as officers. Before being captured, St-Pierre had been a warrant officer for nineteen months and I for thirteen. Barnes had been one for only six months. He was the only one to be promoted. The two guys with the French names didn't get the promotions. We were usually promoted every six months. It was small things like that which made you understand we weren't being treated like the others.

Even if military authorities failed to recognize his long months of imprisonment and promote him to officer rank, they did not make him wait long before sending him back to Canada. "From Bournemouth, I sailed on the *Île de France* to return to Canada. I remember arriving in Halifax on Friday, July 13, 1945. We were amongst the first to come back. The men who wanted to go fight against Japan and we, the prisoners, had priority." The next day, he sent a telegram to his mother to tell her he had arrived and that he would soon have leave to come home.

Cormier's service in the RCAF ended in mid-September 1945 with his demobilization. He had realized his dream of being an aviator, but his imprisonment in *Stalag* IVb in Mühlberg considerably upset his experience. "I enjoyed going on raids, but the day I was captured I wanted the war to be over. The war couldn't end soon enough when I was a prisoner. It's funny how you can look like a bum all of a sudden. Even our uniforms were starting to fall apart. It was discouraging because you hadn't enlisted to spend your time in a prisoner of war camp. I lost part of my youth. I was nineteen, I was still a child."

After his demobilization, Laurie Cormier worked for a few months as an air traffic controller. He was then employed by Canadian National until his retirement in 1982. He married Eileen Gaudet in 1951, and they had four children. They lived in Saint-Anselme, an area of Dieppe, New Brunswick. His name is inscribed on the base of a monument near the cenotaph in Dieppe. A park in the Lakeburn area is named in his honour.

Chapter Five

Executed in a Field
The Story of Henri Édouard Dubé

Rue Henri Dubé runs next to the church in the small commune of Olizy, about fifty kilometres northeast of Reims, in France. Is it named after a local hero? No, the street honours a young Canadian airman from New Brunswick who was executed in this small village during the Second World War. The story of Henri Édouard Dubé has been reconstituted from his military personnel file.[23]

As a teenager growing up in Edmundston at the beginning of the 1930s, Henri Dubé dreamed of becoming an aviator. Aviation was still in its infancy in Canada, and flying fascinated young men in search of adventure. Dubé surely could not have imagined that his dream would end up a nightmare in a field in northeast France. Son of Henry J. and Émelie (née Martin) Dubé, Henri was born on July 16, 1917. He attended Edmundston Composite High School, where he completed an advanced course in woodwork, electricity, and mechanical drawing. On May 11, 1934, he tried to enlist in the RCAF. At the time, however, the youngest of Canada's military services was not looking for recruits. The country was in the midst of the Great Depression and the government had reduced funding for the RCAF. His application was filed. He quickly found

---

23   Except where noted, all the information in this chapter comes from Henri Édouard Dubé's file at Library and Archives Canada, RC 24, volume 27417, item 9754, 315 pp.

(left to right) Pilot Officer Henri Dubé's grave in Olizy, France. Street sign in Olizy, France, commemorating Henri Dubé.

Photos by Ronald Cormier

employment at a hotel in Fredericton. In 1937, he moved to Toronto, where he worked as a machinist and assistant welder before returning to Edmundston in 1939 to drive trucks.

The world changed dramatically in September 1939 when war erupted in Europe and Canada joined Britain and France in the fight against Nazi Germany. Dubé wanted to do his part. He made his way to Woodstock, New Brunswick, on October 20, and volunteered for the Carleton and York Regiment. Although the army was actively recruiting, his time with the regiment was short. He was rejected for service, classified category E, not because of health problems but because of his stature. He was small, measuring only 5 feet 3 inches and weighing but 115 pounds. The medical board declared him under minimum height and weight, and he was returned to civilian life on November 29.

A few months later, he left New Brunswick for Baie-Comeau in Quebec, where he found employment as a clerk with the Hudson's Bay Company. He still had dreams of becoming an aviator and of doing his part in the war. On June 4, 1941, he showed up at the RCAF recruiting centre in Quebec City. The twenty-three-year-old had letters of recommendation from his employer and Baie-Comeau's police chief in the hope that they would improve his chances of being accepted. He had been preparing for many months. The letters were dated December 1940. His employer wrote that "he has proved to be a capable, energetic, and trustworthy employee." Police Chief Brunet added that he had known Dubé for a year and that he was "honest, sober, hard-working, and industrious."

It had already been seven years since Dubé first tried to join the air force. In his notes, the recruiting officer described him as "keen, enthusiastic, bilingual, very anxious to join the RCAF, polite, and well mannered. He should do well as a WOAG (wireless operator/air gunner)." The officer realized that his small size was ideal for the cramped fuselage of a bomber. Although his initial medical exam concluded that his legs were "too short for pilot," he was accepted into the RCAF on June 23. Airman Dubé, service number R96579, was sent to No. 1 Manning Depot in Toronto for basic training. He then went to No. 4 Wireless School at Guelph, Ontario, to complete his training as a radio operator. He learned radio communications and Morse code. It was then on to No. 9 Bombing and Gunnery School in Mont-Joli, Quebec, where his training officer noted that he was "respected by his classmates," but that his gunnery skill was only average.

In June 1942, when he was granted extended leave, the young man returned to Edmundston to see his family. He went there for another reason: on June 23, exactly one year after being accepted in the RCAF, he married Rita Roussel, a twenty-three-year-old stenographer from his hometown.

Dubé progressed through the ranks, and before Christmas, while at No. 8 Air Observer School at L'Ancienne-Lorette, Quebec, he was promoted to acting flight sergeant. He was considered a "good NCO, very reliable, hard worker." It was not his last promotion before leaving for England. He was given two weeks' embarkation leave from June 3 to 17, 1943. He took advantage of it to visit his wife and family in Edmundston. They probably could not have imagined that they would never see him

Airman Henri Édouard Dubé soon after enlisting in the RCAF in June 1941. A height chart behind him indicates he stood just under 5'5" (165 cm).

again. While on leave, he learned he had been promoted to warrant officer.

Like all aircrew arriving in England, he had some flying hours but not on bombers. In Canada, he had accumulated fifty, including some at the controls of a Tiger Moth, a two-seat biplane. The new arrivals were sent to an operational training unit to learn to fly in a bomber. Men who had trained together in Canada tried to form aircrews. But it was the pilot who had the last word on who would fly with him. Dubé joined the crew of Flying Officer Willie L'Abbé from Rimouski. A navigator/bombardier and two other gunners completed the crew. Their training on twin-engine Wellingtons lasted twenty-four weeks, during which they honed their skills. They spent countless hours in the air, including night sorties, emergency landings, and bombing practice. But Dubé still needed twelve weeks of training before joining a squadron. From the OTU, it was on to No. 1659 Heavy Conversion Unit, which trained crews for No. 6 Group (RCAF) of Bomber Command at the RAF base in Topcliffe, Yorkshire. It was here, while they finished their training, that they discovered the

Handley Page Halifax Mk. III bomber from No. 425 "Alouette"
Squadron about to take off from its base at Tholthorpe, Yorkshire.
It was the squadron's principal bomber from December 1943 to May 1945.
DND / PL-40557

quirks of the new bomber that would take them on raids. This new aircraft was the Handley Page Halifax Mk. III, a four-engine plane with a crew of seven.

A flight engineer and a mid-upper gunner completed the crew formed at the OTU: Flying Officer Willie L'Abbé, pilot; Warrant Officer Henri Édouard Dubé, wireless operator/air gunner; Flying Officer Thomas George Gravel from Montreal, navigator; Sergeant Joseph William Peter Paul Whelan from Montreal, bombardier; Sergeant Herman Girard from Tecumseh, Ontario, tail gunner; Sergeant Joseph Alfred Michaud from Edmundston, mid-upper gunner; Sergeant Alan Best (RAF) from North Shields, England, flight engineer. Because most of them were French Canadians, they were posted to No. 425 "Alouette" Squadron at the beginning of February 1944. They did not have to travel far because the squadron's base was at Tholthorpe, about ten kilometres from Topcliffe. The squadron had converted to Halifax Mk. IIIs only a few weeks before they arrived.

On March 5, Dubé was promoted to pilot officer and given a new service number: J86139. He was considered an "above average radio operator, very keen in all duties." He and his crew took part in several sorties against targets in Germany and the occupied countries. On April 24, Bomber Command scheduled a night raid against Karlsruhe, an important industrial city along the Rhine. More than six hundred bombers from No. 6 Group RAF, including "Alouette" Squadron, went on this sortie. It was part of the preparations for the Normandy landings. The Allies needed to destroy German factories and the rail system.

During the afternoon, crews were given their target instructions. Before climbing aboard their bombers shortly before sunset, they had time for a meal and to write letters to their families in case they did not return. Dubé was going out on his seventh sortie. The throttles of Halifax LW591 were pushed to the wall, and the bomber slowly gained speed and left the ground at 2140 hours. The aircraft carried 13,000 pounds of bombs. Their target was some 880 kilometres away as the crow flies. The bomber slowly gained altitude and set course for the English Channel. Problems, however, began shortly afterwards. The details were related by the pilot, Willie L'Abbé, when he returned from a German POW camp a year later, in May 1945.

> After we had been flying for an hour or so, the flight engineer called my attention to our high consumption of petrol. Having had the same experience with the same aircraft a few nights previously, we decided upon continuing for some time longer and if it increased as we went on, we'd turn back and return to field. However, we slowed down our speed, decreased our revs and stopped climbing. We were at 16,000 feet. We carried on like this across the Channel and on to enemy territory.[24] After an hour or so, the flight engineer called again reminding me of a petrol leak in the starboard outer engine.... We flew on to the target, approaching somewhat late. We encountered the aircraft from the

---

24   The May 1945 report by Flying Officer J.W. L'Abbé was found on a discussion forum at www.network54.com/Forums, which is no longer accessible.

second wave coming back head on as they had been briefed, so I decided to circle the target three times until they had all passed before going in to bomb.

Their bombs dropped, L'Abbé set course for England but their problems got worse.

By that time the petrol was very low, so I feathered the starboard outer, decreased height to 12,000 feet....On the way we encountered icing that froze the trimming tabs and caused great vibrations to the aircraft flying on for a few minutes....I tried to climb above icing, unsuccessfully, so I decreased height and as a result of this the instruments froze. The shudder increased and the controls became very stiff and hard to handle. At this time, we were below safety height of the country we were in, handling became impossible, and [the] diving rate increased. I gave the order to bail out and it was carried out successfully. Turning the aircraft toward Germany as the crew was bailing out, I abandoned the aircraft at approximately five hundred to one thousand feet, still in the clouds and rain.

The Halifax bomber hit the ground shortly afterwards. According to German archives, the aircraft crashed at 0200 hours on April 25 in a wooded area near Obersgegen, 195 kilometres northwest of their target at Karlsruhe. Three members of the crew were captured nearby: L'Abbé, the pilot, Gravel, the bombardier, and Girard, the tail gunner. But there was no sign of Dubé, Michaud, Whelan, or Best. Dubé, in fact, was safe and sound. He had parachuted near the village of Berdorf, in Luxembourg, fifteen kilometres south of the crash site. Luck smiled on him. He was quickly taken charge of by a woman from the village, Hélène Raas. She put him in touch with the local resistance chief, Narcisse Lutz.

Meanwhile, in Edmundston, Henri's wife and parents got the dreaded telegram on April 28 that Dubé had been missing since the 25th. In a letter sent to his father a few days later, the casualties officer tried to

Henri Dubé's journey

1. Berdorf, Luxembourg, where he landed and was taken in charge by the resistance;
2. Remoiville, Belgium, where he was hidden by a gamekeeper;
3. Sibret, Belgium, where he was hidden in a resistance camp;
4. Chênet, Belgium, where he found his two crewmates;
5. Charleville, France, where he was captured by the Germans;
6. Olizy, France, where he was executed by the Germans.

Ronald Cormier / Mike Bechthold

be reassuring: "This does not mean that your son has been killed or wounded. He might have parachuted in enemy territory and been taken as a prisoner of war. I have addressed requests for information with the International Red Cross and other organizations which might provide me detail on his fate." Dubé's name did not appear on the list of the missing until five weeks later. The news of his disappearance could be made public but no details on his squadron or the operation could be released. A few days later, the commanding officer of 425 Squadron, Wing Commander McLernon, wrote to Dubé's wife: "In losing this aircraft, we lost one of our best crews which was heading for a brilliant future in the squadron." He added that her husband had already taken part in six sorties over enemy territory.

No one knew Dubé was safe with the resistance in Luxembourg. His coordinates were sent to London by radio, and the resistance kept an eye on him until his identity could be confirmed. A few days later, dressed in civilian clothes, Narcisse Lutz guided him through the Ardennes Forest to Remoiville, near Bastogne, on the other side of the border in Belgium. On May 6, Jean Vincent, the parish priest in Remoiville and a member of the resistance, received confirmation that Dubé was who he claimed to be. He was to bring the airman to a camp in the woods, but Lutz learned that the Germans were surrounding the place. For his own safety, Dubé was hidden by Alphonse Flamant, the local gamekeeper, until the Allies landed in Normandy on June 6. The next day, accompanied by members of the resistance, he was led a short distance to a camp in Sibret. As they entered the woods, they confronted a German patrol and gunfire was exchanged. Dubé escaped and arrived safely at camp.

Dubé was impatient. He didn't want to wait for the Allies to arrive. He befriended a young French student named Hives who was also fleeing the Germans. They studied maps of Belgium and France with the aim of trying to reach Allied lines, which were still some four hundred kilometres away. The two men left, and shortly afterwards arrived at a camp near Chênet, about ten kilometres south of Sibret. Dubé, who hadn't seen a familiar face in weeks, must have been glad to see two of his crew arrive on June 12. Sergeant Alan Best, the navigator, and Sergeant Joseph Alfred

Michaud, the mid-upper gunner and friend from Edmundston, had also been helped by the resistance. Both were nearly captured by the Gestapo in Luxembourg in mid-May but escaped and hid in the area. Michaud was slightly wounded in the head during their confrontation with the Germans.

Many other Allied airmen shot down over occupied territory were also on the run in Belgium and France. Those hidden by clandestine organizations were brought into an escape network known as the Comet Line. Such was the case of First Lieutenant Richard Francis Noble from Gadsden, Alabama, who was a bomber pilot with the United States Army Air Force.[25] His B-17, nicknamed "Lucky Lady," was hit by anti-aircraft fire during a raid against Brux, Czechoslovakia, on May 12. The aircraft was more than four hundred kilometres from its base in England when the ten members of the crew were forced to bail out southeast of Liège, Belgium. Noble and his co-pilot, Second Lieutenant Daniel Viafore, arrived at the Chênet camp in July.

Dubé, who had been on the run for three months, was still trying to reach Allied lines in Normandy. He was not the only man in the camp who had had enough of waiting, but the camp leader, who went by the name of "Gustav," was reluctant to let them leave for fear they might give away the hiding place if captured by the Germans. He had their belongings confiscated and threatened to shoot anyone who tried to get away. But a day later he changed his mind. On July 26, Dubé tried to convince his crewmate, Alan Best, to go with him, but Best refused. He was more successful with the American pilot, Richard Noble. The two men, accompanied by a guide, left the camp at the end of July. He took them to Charleville (now Charleville-Mézières) on the other side of the French border, some sixty kilometres away, and handed them over to a contact from the resistance, Roger Mathieu, who was to take them to another safe location in the escape network. Both airmen spent an hour at Mathieu's house, then the three headed out down the road. They did not get very far before they were stopped by the Germans. Mathieu was

---

25   In 1944, the American air force was part of the Army. It became a separate arm, the United States Air Force, in September 1947.

immediately thrown in prison and was executed by the Germans on August 29.

Dubé and Noble, who were in civilian clothes, had false identity papers as well as Belgian and French currency. They were put on a train under armed guard heading for a POW camp in Germany. It is not known exactly where or when (probably between Charleville and Bastogne), but they managed to escape from the train. They were now at large, and German patrols were at their heels. On August 6, they reached the small hamlet of Falaise, in the Argonne Forest in France. They offered cigarettes to men working in a field, and Dubé asked them for information on the resistance. The farmhands suspected they might be German agents because of Dubé's strange French accent. They told them to go to Grandpré, about ten kilometres away, but, two days later, they had covered only half the distance.

Someone had alerted the Germans, and patrols were sent out to track down the two men in the nearby woods. They were captured around eight o'clock in the morning in an abandoned First World War trench near the small commune of Olizy. They were taken to the local church and chained to the stair railing. They were brought inside one by one, questioned, and beaten. The villagers living near the church could hear their groans. At around four o'clock, they were stuffed into a German military vehicle, which took a dead-end road toward a field known as "Le Canapé." Sometime later, two shots rang out, and the German vehicle left the commune.

Claude Citerne, a ten-year-old boy, heard the shots and headed to the field, where he discovered two bodies. He ran to inform adults in the village, and around 8 p.m., two villagers, Charles Arthur Brion and Lucien Honoré Hubert, made their way to the site, where they surveyed the gruesome scene. The bodies were in a shallow grave covered with leaves. Their heads and bound hands were visible. Both had bullet holes in the middle of the forehead from a revolver shot at close range. The scene led the Frenchmen to believe that the dead men were forced to dig their own graves and were buried alive before being executed. The two bodies were taken to the town hall. The next day, town officials issued

In this 1988 photo, Claude Citerne shows where he found
the two bodies (marked by a cross) on August 8, 1944.

Photo courtesy of Daniel Servais, mayor of Olizy-Primat from 1995 to 2008

death certificates for the two unknown men. Detailed descriptions of the
bodies and their clothes were noted. One was described as being about
twenty years old and measured 5 feet 4 inches, the other about twenty-five
and measuring 5 feet 10 inches. They were buried next to the church,
their graves simply identified as graves six and seven.

In the meantime, Henri Dubé's wife and parents were still trying to
find out what happened to him, but the authorities were at a loss to give
them any information. A report indicating that he had been seen alive in
England in mid-September turned out to be false. His two fellow crew
members, Joseph Alfred Michaud and Alan Best, who had stayed hidden
with the resistance in Belgium, were liberated by advancing American
troops and arrived in England on September 11, 1944. They conveyed
the information they had about Dubé. The last time they had seen him
was at the end of July, when he and Noble left the camp at Chênet. There
was a lot of correspondence between the family and the RCAF. Finally,
on July 18, 1946, more than two years after he went missing, they were
informed that "his death will now be presumed for official purposes to
have occurred on November 6, 1944." The casualty notification noted that
it was also the date chosen by American authorities for the presumptive

declaration of death of Richard Noble. It added that the inquiry to find Henri "will be pursued from every angle."

The search lasted another two years. On April 21, 1948, a team from the American Graves Registration Service arrived in Olizy, and the mystery was finally solved. After graves six and seven were opened, the investigators examined the remains in grave seven. After many weeks, with the help of dental records, they identified them as those of Henri Dubé. They noted that he was missing four front teeth and that they "were lost about the time of death." This finding confirmed that the Germans had beaten him in the church before his execution. There was a more conclusive clue: one testicle was missing from the body. This observation was confirmed by his army medical in November 1939, which noted that his left testicle was surgically removed following an accident in 1938. The former mayor and the communal secretary, who had buried the bodies nearly four years before, identified Henri from a photograph. The boyhood dream of a young man from Edmundston to become an aviator had been snuffed out brutally and tragically at age twenty-seven in a field in France.

Dental records confirmed that the remains in grave six were those of Richard Noble. At the time of the burial of the two men, local authorities had kept a few items as evidence, among which was a wedding band inscribed "B.B.N. TO R.F.N. 6-23-1942." Betty Bradford Nicholson married Richard Francis Noble on June 23, 1942, in Etowa County, Alabama.[26] That date was also important in Henri Dubé's personal history: it too was the day on which he had married Rita Roussel in Edmundston. Two men, one Canadian and one American, living more than two thousand kilometres from each other, were married on the same day, and were executed side by side in a field near the small village of Olizy, France.

After four years, Dubé's wife and parents finally knew that he was a victim of war. In January 1949, the family was sent pictures of his grave, and a permanent headstone was later installed by the Commonwealth War Graves Commission in the cemetery next to the church in Olizy. The

---

26 The date of the marriage was confirmed by Nancy Dupree of the Alabama Department of Archives and History in an email to the author on November 5, 2018.

Memorial to Henri E. Dubé and Richard F. Noble, Olizy, France.

Photo by Ronald Cormier

body of First Lieutenant Noble was transferred to the Ardennes American Cemetery near Neupré, Belgium.

The memory of the two Allied aviators who were savagely executed by the Germans on August 8, 1944, remains alive in Olizy today. The street parallel to the church bears the name of Henri Dubé, the one in front that of Richard Noble. A memorial in their honour was erected in front of the church in 2000.

Chapter Six

Dieppe, August 19, 1942
The Story of John Arsenault

"I sacrificed two years and eight months of my life in a prisoner of war camp and it wasn't my fault. I would have changed places with a soldier on the front lines but it wasn't possible." This quote sums up the experiences of John Arsenault, a young Acadian from Adamsville, New Brunswick, who was taken prisoner at Dieppe, France, on August 19, 1942. Half a century after the tragic Dieppe raid, he was still reticent to talk about what he went through. He agreed to tell his story anonymously. In the original French language version of this book, *Entre bombes et barbelés*, the author respected John Arsenault's wish. He had never spoken of his experiences to most of his closest friends. After publication of the book, however, he began telling his story. John's widow, Agnès, consented to the publication of his name after his death in this edition of the story.

John Arsenault attended Sainte-Anne College in Church Point, Nova Scotia, in the 1930s, but had to abandon his studies to help his family after his father's death. Unlike most young men his age, Arsenault had a good job in the summer of 1940, but that did not stop him from volunteering for military service. Since he was the main breadwinner for his family, he could have asked for a deferral, but, for him, there was no question of doing so. He travelled to Halifax to join the Royal Canadian Navy, but there was no room, so he chose the army instead.

John Arsenault shortly after
his enlistment in 1940.
Courtesy of Richard Arsenault

I got a job at Canadian National in 1934. I was working in
Edmundston at the time. I left my employment to join the army
in June 1940. I was twenty-five years old. I was a bit older than the
majority of those who were enrolling. I chose to go with the Royal
Canadian Engineers. Two days after leaving port, they announced
over the ship's speaker that, according to the Germans, the
Duchess of York had been sunk. It was funny because we were still
on it. The crossing took twenty-eight days. It was February 1942.
There were many ships and we had to stay in convoy. We were
quite far north in the Atlantic to avoid German submarines. A lot
of the guys were seasick, especially those from the Prairies. Me, I
wasn't sick, but nearly. They confined us inside and we couldn't
go out for four or five days because the seas were too rough.

Arsenault was sent to the 7th Field Company, Royal Canadian Engineers, after arriving in England. He continued his training in the handling of explosives and became a sapper. His unit was posted to Eastbourne on the south coast.

By the beginning of 1942, the Allies had showed little success against Hitler's armies on the continent. Adding to these poor results, Soviet leader Joseph Stalin was clamouring for the opening of a second front in the West to force Hitler to withdraw troops that were at Moscow's door. The Americans, who had only been involved in the conflict since December 1941, were also putting pressure on the British prime minister to launch an assault on the continent. Churchill was well aware that the Allies were not ready for an offensive against occupied Europe, that they didn't have the arms or the manpower needed for such a venture. He believed, however, that operations against the Germans were needed to relieve pressure on the Soviet Union.

Morale among the thousands of Canadian troops in England, some of whom had been there for more than two years without seeing action, was beginning to wane. Soldiers from most other Commonwealth countries were already fighting, notably in North Africa. In February, Lieutenant-General Harry Crerar, in temporary command of Canadian forces in Britain,[27] lobbied for the participation of Canadians in operations against the enemy at the first possible opportunity.[28] Canadian military and political leaders were more than pleased for the opportunity to send them into combat. It is in this context that Operation Rutter, a raid against the port of Dieppe, in Normandy, was born. The assault, planned by Combined Operations under Lord Louis Mountbatten, cousin of King George VI, was to be undertaken by a group of about five hundred British commandos. The Canadian request to be involved in a future operation against occupied Europe presented a new option. Why not mount a massive raid of five or six thousand men instead? Churchill quickly rallied behind the idea of a raid in force against Dieppe. Canadian military leaders saw this operation as a means to boost troop morale and

---

27   The senior commander, Lieutenant-General Andrew McNaughton, was on convalescent leave in Canada.
28   Letter from Crerar to General Montgomery, commander of South-Eastern Command, dated February 5, 1942.

give them combat experience. The privilege of taking part in the first large-scale raid against occupied France fell to the 2nd Canadian Infantry Division. Major-General John Hamilton Roberts was given command of the land forces.

On May 20, 1942, Arsenault and the 7th Field Company left for training on the Isle of Wight. The men did not know these exercises were to prepare them for Operation Rutter. The raid against Dieppe was scheduled for June 21, but the planners decided to postpone it after the preparatory exercises turned out to be a failure. The operation got the green light after a second rehearsal and the raid was rescheduled for July 4. "In July [on the 3rd], we boarded ships for the attack on Dieppe. After four days, we disembarked because they feared the Germans had gotten wind of the operation. We returned to Horsham [in Sussex]."

Adverse weather conditions continued until July 8, forcing the cancellation of the raid. The men were warned not to talk about it. British authorities feared the Germans had learned of the plans for the assault because the German air force had attacked some of the troopships in the ports. This might have led one to conclude that Combined Operations would abandon the operation, but such was not the case. A few days after the cancellation, the raid was reborn under a new code name, Jubilee. The idea was put forward by Captain John Hughes-Hallett, naval commander of the operation. At Combined Operations, some people believed that, even if the Germans had gotten wind of the cancelled raid, they would never think that anyone would be so foolish as to remount it against the same target. The plans for the assault were modified slightly but the objective remained the same: Dieppe. The task was assigned to nearly five thousand men from the 2nd Canadian Infantry Division, two British commandos, a Royal Marine Commando, and the 10th Inter-Allied commando, which included fifty American Rangers. The raid was scheduled to take place after sunrise on August 19.

More than three hundred men of the Royal Canadian Engineers boarded ships at Newhaven, Sussex, on August 18. Most believed they were going on another exercise. It was only after they were at sea that they learned their objective was again Dieppe. The men were worried.

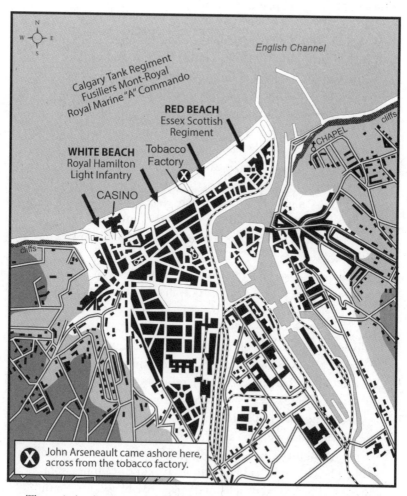

The main landing beaches of the Dieppe raid. John Arsenault came ashore at the spot marked with an X across from the tobacco factory.

Ronald Cormier / Mike Bechthold

Arsenault and the others were asking themselves if the Germans had knowledge of the raid planned for July.

We left around eight o'clock on the evening of the eighteenth. It was already dark. We had to land at low tide and wait for it to rise to float the barges to return to England. It was 5:20 when we arrived in front of Dieppe. We had been told we were going to Dieppe to destroy the port where ships were unloaded.

The Germans were ready because they had detected our ships. There was a small battle[29] at sea against German ships when we crossed the Channel. One or two infantry units had already come ashore before we got there. We were in landing craft with the tanks of the Calgary Regiment. There were three tanks and us on the ship; we were on the sides. Guys were falling all over the place when I landed. I had forty or forty-five pounds of explosives on my back.

We landed first, then the tanks came out. They didn't get far because there were stone and brick walls about ten feet high. We were facing the centre of town. The beaches were covered with large chert pebbles which made it difficult for the tanks to advance. The Germans let the first two units in, the South Saskatchewan Regiment[30] and the Royal Hamilton Light Infantry. We went in with the Essex Scottish on Red Beach, not far from the casino. There was a tobacco factory with a tall chimney across from where we were. The beaches were well fortified with artillery hidden everywhere. The Churchill tanks were equipped with six-pounder guns which were only good at less than a thousand yards. The Germans had big cannons two or three miles from the coast. They could do a lot of damage. We blew a hole in the seawall to allow the tanks to go through. I was armed with a Sten

---

29   Shortly before 4:00 a.m. on the morning of August 19, a short naval engagement took place between escort ships of a German convoy heading to Dieppe and ships accompanying British commandos heading to the beach at Berneval.

30   The South Saskatchewan Regiment landed at Pourville, about three kilometres southwest of Dieppe, but was part of the same group of landing craft heading toward the main beach at Dieppe.

Dieppe, August 20, 1942, the day after the raid. Tanks of the
Calgary Regiment bear witness to the futility of the assault. It is across
from the tobacco factory with the two chimneys (marked with a
white X at top right) that John Arsenault was captured.

gun, which was only good to fight in a room. I picked up a rifle on
the beach. There were Bren gunners with us, but they couldn't do
much because the Germans were firing from all sides. The worst
things were the grenades and the mortars we heard coming.

The exploding grenades and mortars projected deadly fragments of chert
stones that killed and wounded men all along the beach. "I remember
a destroyer going along the coast firing its large guns. I could see the
flames coming out of its cannons. The ship was firing behind Dieppe on
German reinforcements which were coming. It was at least a mile and a
half offshore."

Farther out in the English Channel, a Royal Navy destroyer, HMS
Calpe, served as headquarters for the raid's commander. Major-General
Roberts received a garbled message that led him to believe that Canadians

were making headway in Dieppe. The land force commander sent in his floating reserve, Les Fusiliers Mont-Royal, into the fray to exploit what seemed to be a breakthrough. The situation, however, was quite different. The Canadians were decimated by heavy enemy fire. When Roberts realized this, he ordered the evacuation of the beaches at around 9:30.

When the order came, Arsenault had a difficult choice to make. He could see the landing craft that were to take them back to England. He could try to cross the beach under murderous enemy fire and swim one or two hundred metres to the craft or he could stay hidden and wait to be taken prisoner. "It was about two o'clock in the afternoon when the white flag went up. The Germans didn't waste any time in coming. I was still on the beach along the seawall because we hadn't been able to move from there. I was tired."

Arsenault had spent only a few hours in combat. For him, the war was over and a new experience had begun. Along with 1,945 other Canadians, he was captured by the Germans, who gloated over the failure of their adversaries.

The Germans made us come out and paraded us through Dieppe to the hospital courtyard. When we were being led through the streets of Dieppe, French people tried to help us but the Germans stopped them. They shoved old women who came to the road to give us apples, potatoes, and things like that. They hit them with the butts of their rifles. It wasn't funny. We walked until seven or eight o'clock that night. We spent two or three weeks in a large field surrounded by barbed wire. They later loaded us in boxcars and we headed for Germany. The trip took five or six days. There were only two small window openings in the boxcars and the doors were locked. We were between 80 and 100 per car. We were only given something to drink once or twice during the trip. The train stopped a couple of times and the Germans put a pail of water in the boxcar. We drank from it.

This photo of German origin shows captured Canadian soldiers on their way to POW camps under armed escort in the streets of Dieppe on August 19, 1942. Some are barefoot, others lightly wounded, and most seem demoralized. Canadian War Museum/ CWM 19900076-952 George Metcalf Archival Collection

The train arrived in Lamsdorf, in Upper Silesia, a part of southwest Poland annexed by Germany in 1939, where *Stalag* VIIIb was located. Used during the First World War, the camp had a bad reputation. Arsenault would get to know this camp very well over the next twenty-seven months.

> We arrived at the camp in the evening but they waited until daybreak to let us out. We marched to the camp. They searched us before we went in. You only kept the clothes on your back. The camp was located in a large treeless field. There were two or three fences about fifteen feet from each other. They were about fifteen feet high and topped with barbed wire. There were towers all around the camp with machine guns and two or three men. Other prisoners were already there when we arrived, men captured in North Africa. There were British, Australians, and

New Zealanders. At the beginning, they separated us from the others. We were nearly two thousand Canadians. The barracks were made of cement blocks with cement floors. They were only one storey. There were rows of three-tiered beds along its whole length. There was a little coal furnace in the middle but coal was rare. Our beds were straw mattresses. We had two blankets. In summer, it was too hot, and in winter, too cold.

What we missed most at the beginning was food because we noticed it more. You had to accept the idea you were a prisoner until something happened. If you couldn't adapt, you suffered. We got our coffee as soon as we got up in the morning. That's all we got in the morning. The coffee arrived in an old barrel carried by two guys. We got our bread around 4:00 in the afternoon. We divided a loaf among four or five guys and we ate it with a bit of cheese. At the end, the food wasn't very good because the Allies bombed the railroads. All the parcels from the Red Cross went through Berne, Switzerland. The Germans gave us potatoes and sometimes pork, fat, and cheese, the "fish cheese." When that cheese left the cookhouse two hundred yards away, you could see the flies coming and you knew what you were getting to eat. There was also cabbage soup. They tied a cabbage to a string and dipped it in a barrel of water. When the soup barrel arrived, we searched the bottom to find what was in it. We plunged our arm to the bottom but found no more cabbage there than on top.

In early October 1942, about a month after the Canadians arrived in Lamsdorf, the Germans took reprisals against the men captured at Dieppe. This decision followed the discovery of the operational plans for the raid. In the section on intelligence, it was written that German prisoners were to have their hands shackled as a security measure. The Germans considered this directive as contrary to the Hague Convention on the treatment of prisoners of war, and they retaliated by tying the hands of those captured at Dieppe. Arsenault and the other POWs suffered this fate from October 8, 1942, until November 21, 1943. Their hands were shackled from eight in the morning to eight in the evening.

Not long after we arrived at camp, they put us in chains. At the beginning, they tied us with rope. Then they put us in handcuffs with a chain between the two wrists. The chain was long enough to put our hands in our pockets. If it had been shorter, it would have been quite inconvenient to go to the toilet. After a while, we found a way to get rid of those cuffs. We were supposed to wear them when we played cards in the barracks. There was always a guy at each door to warn us if a German was coming. One day, we became aware of a German behind us watching us play. We were taken, the four of us, and brought to the office. They made us stand on the porch with our noses against the wall of the building. It wasn't long before your head hit the wall. They kept us there for three or four hours. If you had the misfortune to back away from the wall, they gave you a swift kick in the behind. It was our duty to cause them grief.

The morale of the Dieppe prisoners in Lamsdorf didn't flinch during the thirteen months of this ordeal. Quite to the contrary, they played a game of wits with the Germans. They removed their chains as soon as guards were out of sight and caused them all sorts of problems when the time came to put the cuffs on their wrists in the morning. Even shackled, they scored a moral victory against the enemy. The Germans finally ended the practice after the Canadian government threatened to chain the thousands of Germans who were in POW camps in Canada.

By the beginning of their second year of imprisonment at *Stalag* VIIIb, the Canadians never missed an opportunity to defy the Germans. They realized that the tide of war had turned in favour of the Allies and liberation was only a question of time.

When the bombers returned from Italy or went out on bombing raids against refineries in daytime, we were outside cheering them on. The guards had large dogs they let go in the camp. We hurried to the safety of our barracks. We had news from the BBC. A radio was hidden in one of the barracks, and we got the news from a guy who came to our barrack to tell us what was happening. If the Germans suspected we had news from the radio, they cut off the power and searched the barracks. They nearly destroyed the barrack to try to find it, but never found where it was hidden. We also got a little newspaper, a leaflet which came from Berlin. The Germans gave us the news they wanted us to hear. It was all the opposite of what we heard on the BBC.

Liberation, however, even if it was in the daily thoughts of the prisoners, was not their main preoccupation. The meagre rations did not do much to quell their hunger. Those, like Arsenault, who had the opportunity to get a bit more food didn't hesitate to seize it.

Because I was a corporal, I didn't have to work but I volunteered to work in a sugar factory for three or four months. We processed sugar from sugar beets. It wasn't refined, it was yellow. That's where I learned they made sugar from beets. They were the size of turnips. I had never seen that before. They went through a machine. We put bags under a chute and filled them. About thirty of us worked there. We always brought back some sugar to the camp but it wasn't very good. It tasted like turnip even if it was sweet.

Our rations were a bit better there than in camp. If you got one or two potatoes in camp, you'd get three at the plant. They also made efforts to give us our Red Cross parcels. We divided them in four, which wasn't bad. There was a pound of butter, a can of jam, a quarter pound of cheese, biscuits, raisins, prunes, a can of sardines, and one of salmon. It weighed from ten to twelve pounds. We preferred the Canadian Red Cross parcel because we were more used to it. It had more variety than the others. I'd sometimes open a can of salmon, eat half and store the rest under my bed for two or three days before eating what was left. I did that more than once and never got food poisoning. I wouldn't do that today. Four guys would save their potatoes for two or three days. We boiled them and threw in a can of salmon. We mixed everything together and divided it in four. It was tasty, it was good! There was a large chocolate bar in our Red Cross parcels. If you gave it to a German soldier, he would bring you parts for a radio, eggs, or other things.

But the Red Cross chocolate bar was not the main currency of exchange in the camp, as Arsenault remembered.

If you were ready to sacrifice your cigarettes, you could trade them for all sorts of things. When a man got cigarettes from home, he was notified to go get them at the post office. They opened the packages, took out the cigarettes, and broke them in two. They put them back in the paper and gave them to you like that. They were afraid something might be hidden in them. It was rare one got a cigarette which wasn't broken in two. I know I didn't get all the cigarettes sent to me. The Germans kept a lot because the guys from Canadian National sent me a lot, up to a thousand at a time.

The POWs at *Stalag* VIIIb who did not work didn't know what to do with their free time. There were a few organized activities, and most dreamt of freedom.

We played cards to pass the time and when we had been "good boys" we were allowed to play softball. We played cards a lot. We had tournaments: Cribbage, Auction 45, Two Hundred, and Bridge. There was a guy from Toronto, Percy Ross, who had played accordion with an orchestra. He got an accordion from the Red Cross the last year we were in camp. He played music all the time. We had mass every Sunday since there were one or two priests in the camp.

I often thought of trying to escape. It was futile because we didn't have any maps. If you had learned geography, you knew the Alps were in such and such a direction but you didn't know the people in those countries. If you escaped and someone asked you a question, you were lost. They dug an escape tunnel in one of the other barracks, but I don't know if anyone made it out or not. I remember it was hard to find a place to get rid of the dirt dug out from the tunnels.

After twenty-seven months behind barbed wire, Arsenault left *Stalag* VIIIb along with hundreds of other Canadian prisoners. Departing the camp, however, did not mean their immediate freedom, only the beginning of a new and difficult ordeal, once again conducted by German guards.

On December 22, 1944, we left the camp and began marching west. We could hear the big Russian guns firing in the distance. We marched, marched, and marched some more. We walked from December 22 to March 17. During all that time, we went only one day without marching. We walked from ten to twelve miles a day. We went from one military district to another. The guards changed all the time. What we found hardest was food. We hadn't been able to bring any with us because we didn't have any advance notice we were leaving.

It was winter and the weather was nasty. It sometimes snowed and other times we had rain. You were always soaked and your feet were wet. We slept in fields at night. We didn't sleep more than three or four times in barns. We slept on the ground, three or four together. We put a blanket down, lay on it, and covered ourselves with the other three blankets. If a guy turned around, everyone had to turn. The Germans buried their turnips and potatoes in mounds of earth. Some men tried to get some but the Germans shot at them. The guys knew they had to come back. I never saw anyone being killed. They put a sign on guys who were weak and left them on the side of the road. In the morning, some of them couldn't get up.

The survivors of this march over hundreds of kilometres across occupied territories and regions of Germany waited about a month and a half before being freed at the end of April 1945.

We were liberated about fifty miles south of Hanover. It was the British [Second British Army] who liberated us. We were in a camp. There was no barbed wire around it even if there were not enough buildings to house everyone. We hadn't been there long before the Allies arrived. The camp was in a hollow surrounded by hills. There weren't too many Germans around, only a few guards. Everything got quiet around eleven o'clock or midnight the night before our liberation. We couldn't hear anything. There were no rifle shots, no planes. We were a bit worried because there had always been a lot of noise around us. We were afraid to fall asleep because it was too peaceful. In the morning, we saw tanks around the camp. We didn't know if they were Germans or Allies.

Around 8 o'clock, a British reconnaissance vehicle drove up to the gate. There must have been about a dozen [soldiers] in it. The Germans were waiting, all lined up, and they dropped their weapons. An Englishman got out and shot the padlock off the gate. They came in and took the Germans out. There were four or five old horses tied behind a large cookhouse where they prepared the meals. We had them for dinner the next day. We were twenty-four thousand prisoners in the camp. At 4 o'clock in the afternoon, we each had a loaf of white bread. Was it ever good!

We stayed in camp for another three or four days. One morning, we climbed aboard trucks and travelled about eighty miles to an airfield where we boarded planes for England. I had only been back in England a short time when the war ended. I spent about a month in hospital in England. I weighed only 105 pounds when I got there. I had lost about thirty pounds in camp. They

gave us a lot of milk, cheese, and other things to fatten us up.
When I got back to Canada [in July 1945], I weighed 147 pounds.

Arsenault was demobilized in August 1945 and he returned to Moncton, where he resumed his employment with Canadian National. "From twenty-five to thirty, those are the best years of one's life. I lost them to a certain point because at CN some of the men got promoted when I was away. In spite of that, I can't complain." He did not regret those years, but he never forgave those who sent him to risk his life at Dieppe. "I always said to myself that they had used me as a guinea pig because I had failed to enter Dieppe and get out."

John Arsenault worked nearly forty years for Canadian National before retiring in 1974. He married Agnès Cormier on August 19, 1946, four years to the day after he was taken prisoner in Dieppe. He wanted the date to remind him of happier days, not just his few hours in combat. The couple had four children and lived in Moncton. Arsenault's name is inscribed on the base of a monument near the cenotaph in Dieppe.

After the publication of the original French-language version of this book, *Entre bombes et barbelés*, the author presented Arsenault with a copy. The veteran explained that he did not want his name published because he was ashamed of having been captured at Dieppe, because his war had lasted only a few hours. After reading his story, he kept the book on his coffee table and told friends who visited him that he was in it. His wife later told the author that the book had changed him, that he could finally talk about his experiences, and that he was free of the nightmare he had lived through half a century earlier.

Chapter Seven

"Like a load of pigs"
The Story of Alcide Gallant

The prisoner of war camp at Moosburg an der Isar, northeast of Munich, held about twenty thousand men at the beginning of 1945. The few hundred Canadian POWs already at *Stalag* VIIa were about to be joined by a young Acadian from Prince Edward Island. Alcide Gallant, from Abrams Village, was captured by the Germans in mid-January near the Arielli River, north of Ortona, on the Adriatic coast of Italy.

Like most of his contemporaries, Gallant saw the army as a way to make a new life.

I left home when I was fourteen. I didn't even have a suitcase. I put my things in a potato sack and left. It was during the Depression, there was no work. My first job was on a farm. I worked from morning till night for my room and board. Once in a while, they gave me an old pair of coveralls which were pretty patched up. When I tried to join the army the first time, I wasn't the minimum age [eighteen]. I was a year too young. I went back the following week. I had aged a year in the space of a week. They took me. It was in Charlottetown. I did my basic training there. I was then sent to Camp Borden, Ontario, for advanced training. I crossed to England on the *Queen Elizabeth* on October 2, 1942.

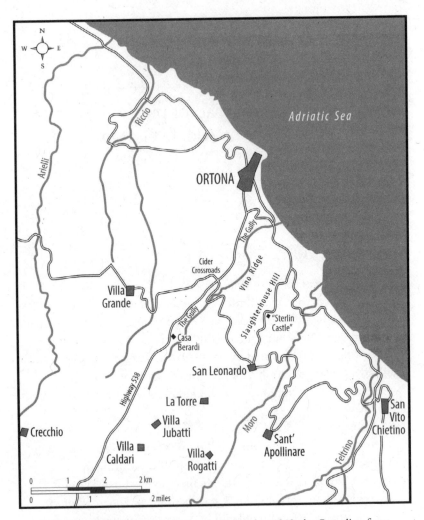

After the bloody fighting at Ortona in December 1943, the Canadian front became static except for a few raids, including the one against German defences along the Arielli River, where Alcide Gallant was captured on January 16, 1944. Ronald Cormier / Mike Bechthold

Gallant was then serving with the Princess Louise Fusiliers, an infantry regiment from Halifax, but shortly after arriving in England he was transferred to the Perth Regiment of the 11th Canadian Infantry Brigade of 5th Canadian Armoured Division. "I went to Italy in November 1943, about a year after I got to England. The Perth Regiment was from Stratford, Ontario. A few of the guys spoke French. They had been transferred from other regiments. We arrived at the front in the Arielli area, north of Ortona, at the end of 1943." 1st Canadian Infantry Division had just won the bloody battle of Ortona, a small Adriatic port defended by elite German troops from 1st Parachute Division. The fighting from December 20 to 28 had reduced most of the town of ten thousand inhabitants to ashes.

On the night of January 13/14, 11th Canadian Infantry Brigade relieved elements of 1st Canadian Division at the front. For Gallant and the Perth Regiment, it was their first encounter with the enemy and, for many of them, it was their last.

The fighting didn't last very long for me but things got hot while it lasted. The first thing you do when you get into combat is soil your pants. After that, you get used to it, you get used to it. I never thought I'd be killed. I said to myself that if I was killed, the game would be over. Bullets were flying by my head...zoom, zoom. I hadn't been in combat for long before I was taken prisoner on January 16, 1944. We were in an olive grove, lying down in a ditch between the rows of trees. When the Germans fired, the bullets flew over our heads because we were protected by the little ditch. We were caught in a trap, a whole company from our regiment, about 160 men. We had fired all our ammunition. The Germans let us come into their positions, then surrounded us. I was captured in the evening. It was getting dark. I had taken off all my kit and was getting ready to go back to our lines. The Germans were as smart as us. They came to our hiding spot and yelled: *"Raus, Kommen Sie mit Hände hoch!"* ["Come out with your hands up!"]. They stuck their bayonets in our backs.

Soldiers of the Perth Regiment in a trench near Orsogna, Italy, on January 19, 1944, near where Alcide Gallant was captured. By this time, he was already on his way to a POW camp in Germany. LAC / PA-130603

This first clash with an elite unit of the German army, the 3rd Battalion of 1st Parachute Regiment, which had just retreated from Ortona, was very costly for the Perth Regiment. Its losses were forty-seven dead, sixty-two wounded, and twenty-eight captured, including Gallant. Few Canadians escaped from the trap.

The Germans took us to an old building not far from there. When they had enough prisoners, they put us aboard trains for Germany. We were loaded in boxcars. It was like we were like a load of pigs. We were about one hundred per car. At one end, there was straw and, in the middle, a wooden barrel cut in half which served as a toilet. After two or three days, the barrel was full. When the train shunted, the stuff flew from one end of the car to the other. They gave us our ration when we got on the train. They didn't open the doors again until we got to Moosburg. I don't remember exactly how many days it took to reach Germany...six or seven days, I think.

We marched a mile and a half before reaching the camp. The first thing the Germans did was disinfect us because we were covered with lice and fleas. They then sent us to our barrack. What struck me the most when I entered the camp was that I didn't know how long I'd spend in that prison. It wasn't like I knew the length of my sentence. I would only get out when our side won. It wasn't all rosy. There were at least twenty thousand men from all the Allied countries in the camp. There were Americans, British, New Zealanders, and others. The Russians were apart, in another section of the camp, separated from us by a barbed wire fence even higher than the one surrounding ours. There were bunk beds with straw mattresses full of lice. We had a hard time sleeping at night because the lice devoured us. There were no officers in our barrack. They were apart and they didn't have to work like us ordinary soldiers.

In the morning, the guards came to wake us up with dogs. If they had to come in a second time, a guy didn't have time to put on his pants; he went outside in his pyjamas. We got up early to take the train to go to work. First thing was *Appell*. They counted us: "*Eins, zwei, drei, vier* . . ." In German, my prisoner number was *eins, drei, neun, drei, vier, fünf*: 139345. They sent me to work on the railroad near Munich. We had to travel in freight cars from Moosburg to Munich, twenty-five miles away. On our way, we passed not far from the camp at Dachau.[31] We could see prisoners walking. We suspected there was something going on in that camp.

---

31 Dachau, located forty kilometres from Moosburg, was the first concentration camp built by the Nazis in 1933, where thousands of prisoners died of hunger or illness or were executed.

At the beginning, they sent us to repair bomb damage to the rail lines. We were under the bombs because there was bombing nearly every day. Munich was a large rail centre. When the bombing started, we had to run about 100 metres to hide in a ditch. We saw the planes coming, but we didn't have any real shelters. A bomb doesn't always fall on the target. We saw the planes and when one was shot down, we counted the guys bailing out. Sometimes, they all came out; other times, none came out. The Americans bombed the most often. If they bombed on a Saturday, we were sure to go out on Sunday to repair the damage. We worked seven days a week most of the time.

We weren't very well fed. They came with big pots full of turnip leaf soup we called *skilee*. That's all we had to eat at noon. In the morning, we got nothing at all, only our ration…a piece of sour black bread with the date stamped on it. That bread might be seven or eight months old. It looked more like sawdust. At night in camp, we got a ration of two potatoes which were often rotten. If both were, you were out of luck. They stored the potatoes outside under mounds of dirt and straw. What kept you alive were the Red Cross parcels which arrived from time to time. It was hard in winter. We made brews of porridge from the tea and rolled oats in our parcels, but we didn't have a stove. We fabricated what we called "blowers," a sort of small stove made from empty tin cans. It didn't take much to get the water boiling and prepare porridge and tea. Two guys shared because it took less wood to heat. A guy from Miscouche, Prince Edward Island, did his cooking with me. He was quite a bit older. He found it hard and cried a lot.

Hunger was a constant companion in camp, and the prisoners tried to add to their meagre rations. One day, an opportunity presented itself, and Gallant didn't hesitate to seize it.

In the fall of 1944, they came looking for guys to work on farms. They wanted volunteers. I put both hands in the air...volunteer to work on a farm! I told myself that there would be something to eat there. We were two guys working on that farm. We didn't sleep at the farm but at the hotel in the village. There were no guards with us at the farm. They brought us in the morning and came to pick us up in the evening. We were well treated. We worked for a widow. Her husband and her sons had been killed in the war. She had three daughters: twins sixteen or seventeen years old and another who was eighteen. Around ten in the morning, the old woman came to the field with a snack. We took our other meals with the family. The widow had an egg quota which she had to turn over to the government. A guy came to get the eggs every week. I spent about two months on that farm.

These two months presented Gallant and his friend with an opportunity to escape, to try to reach Allied lines in western France or head for neutral Switzerland. Although there were no guards at the farm, the two prisoners were aware of the dangers that awaited them if they tried to escape. Since the summer of 1944, a German warning, posted in all camps, was very clear: "The escape from prison camps is no longer a sport!"

We thought of escaping every day, but we asked ourselves where we might go. We would need civilian clothes, maps, and all sorts of papers. If a guy got caught, he was done for. The men who tried to escape were put in the hole when they were caught. Many were executed on the spot. In our part of the camp, we didn't have time to think about digging escape tunnels because we worked seven days a week.

Living conditions in the POW camps led to conflicts between men who would risk their lives for their comrades in arms on the battlefield. For the most part, prisoners were deprived of news from the outside and contact with their loved ones.

NOTICE
To All Prisoners Of War

— POSTED IN ALL GERMAN PRISONER OF WAR CAMPS —

TO ALL PRISONERS OF WAR!

THE ESCAPE FROM PRISON CAMPS IS NO LONGER A SPORT!

Germany has always kept to the Hague Convention and only punished recaptured prisoners of war with minor disciplinary punishment.

Germany will still maintain these principles of International Law.

But England has besides fighting at the front in an honest manner instituted an illegal warfare in non combat zones in the form of gangster commandos, terror bandits and sabotage troops even up to the frontiers of Germany.

They say in a captured secret and confidential English military pamphlet.

THE HANDBOOK
OF MODERN IRREGULAR
WARFARE:

" . . . The days when we could practise the rules of sportmanship are over. For the time being, every soldier must be a potential gangster and must be prepared to adopt their methods whenever necessary."

"The sphere of operations should always include the enemy's own country, any occupied territory, and in certain circumstances, such neutral countries as he is using as a source of supply."

England has with these instructions opened up a non military form of gangster war!

Germany is determined to safeguard her homeland, and especially her war industry and provisional centres for the fighting fronts. Therefore it has become necessary to create strictly forbidden zones, called death zones, in which all unauthorised trespassers will be immediately shot on sight.

Escaping prisoners of war, entering such death zones, will certainly lose their lives. They are therefore in constant danger of being mistaken for enemy agents or sabotage groups.

URGENT WARNING IS GIVEN AGAINST MAKING FUTURE ESCAPES!
IN PLAIN ENGLISH:
Stay in the camp where you will be safe!
Breaking out of it is now a damned dangerous act.

THE CHANCES OF PRESERVING YOUR LIFE ARE ALMOST NIL!
All police and military guards have been given the most strict orders
to shoot on sight all suspected persons.

ESCAPING FROM PRISON CAMPS HAS CEASED TO BE A SPORT!

German poster warning of the consequences of escaping,
posted in all POW camps in the summer of 1944 following the escape
of seventy-six men from *Stalag Luft* III at Sagan on the night
of March 24/25. The German secret police, the Gestapo, executed
fifty of the airmen who made it out. Collection of Laurie Cormier

The guys didn't have much patience. You had to watch what you said. Everything started the minute we got on the train piled one on top of another. If you shoved someone, you could get punched. The Germans had a sort of newspaper they gave out in the camp, but everything in it was always in their favour. They were always winning and everything was going great. We got most of the real news from newly arrived prisoners. They told us what was going on. From time to time, we could write a short letter to Canada. My wife kept some which had been censored by the Germans. It was quite a while before my parents learned what had happened to me. I had been reported missing for two or three months.

The prisoners had little to help while away their time in camp.

We played cards for cigarettes in the evening, American ones. Some guys didn't smoke. If you were lucky and won lots of cigarettes, you could trade them with German guards for slices of bread or baguettes. It was a sort of black market. At the end, they didn't have much more than us. The Germans treated us well at work as long as we kept working. You couldn't drop your pick or shovel for too long. Most of the guards were crippled or older guys who couldn't do anything else. Our guards were strict but they didn't beat the prisoners. Once you got used to their system of discipline, it wasn't too hard. You followed the system because you had no other choice.

All POWs kept certain images of daily life behind barbed wire in their memory. Gallant remembered one that bears witness to the horrors which often confronted prisoners. "I can still see the scene of two Russians pulling a cart transporting the pot of the famous *skilee* which was served at noon. Each was missing a leg. The two were pulling the cart with only one leg each."

More than fifteen months after Gallant was captured in Italy, the order arrived to evacuate part of *Stalag* VIIa.

Prisoners exercising in Moosburg POW camp. Australian War Memorial / P03138.019

About ten days before the end of the war, they evacuated our part
of the camp. We left on the march. We were heading towards
the Americans advancing in our direction. At night, we slept in
barns in the villages. After marching for five or six days, I saw a
small plane fly over in the afternoon. It was low enough for me
to see the American star on the side. Around nine o'clock that
evening, the guards told us they were running away but that it
was better if we stayed where we were. Around ten or eleven,
we saw the German army retreating, chased by the Americans.
Early next morning, three American tanks arrived. They were
loaded with chocolate bars and cigarettes. They were from
Patton's army [Third US Army]. Our German guards had hidden
in woods about two kilometres from the village. We went with
the Americans to pick them up. They didn't put up a big fight.
The tanks fired a few shots in the woods and white flags began
popping up here and there. Most of the guards had changed into
civilian clothes. We said "*Hallo, Posten*" when we met them.
The Americans called them over and asked for their papers.

It was a big day when the Americans arrived. We celebrated.
Most civilians had left the village we were in. After three or four

days, there were not many cows and pigs left! We ate lots.…
That's where I learned butchering. It took the Americans three
or four days to prepare an airfield to evacuate us. They unrolled
metal mats for the old bombers to land on. From there, we were
flown to France, to Reims. We then climbed aboard DC-3s for
England. We arrived the evening the war ended [May 8]. There
was a lot of celebrating.

We weren't allowed to celebrate. They took us to the hospital for two days of tests. I had lost weight during my sixteen
months in the camp. When I was captured, I weighed nearly 200
pounds. At the end of the war, I was down to 160. We were sent to
Aldershot and given a month's pass after we came out of hospital.
All our pay was due. That was a lot of money in those days. Many
went to London. I think they wanted us to spend our money
before coming back to Canada. When we got back to camp, there
was still no embarkation for Canada, so they sent us on leave for
another two or three weeks. We finally left on the *Queen Mary*.
We landed in New York. From there, I went to Fredericton, where
I was demobilized.

Contrary to what happened in other Acadian regions, the residents of
villages on Prince Edward Island recognized the sacrifices of their sons
who went off to war. "When we came back from the war, there were
receptions in village halls. The guys were asked to say what happened
to them. Not many spoke out." Gallant's experience was divided in two
phases: his few hours in combat and his sixteen months as a prisoner of
war. "It's not every day I can talk about what happened to me during
the war. It's like a dream. I can't believe it's true. The hardest thing was
having lost my youth."

Alcide Gallant married Géralda Cassie from Cocagne, New Brunswick, in 1945, shortly after his return from overseas. The couple raised
fourteen children. He worked as a heavy equipment operator in Ontario
and the Maritimes. He retired in 1975. After spending a few years on
Prince Edward Island, the couple moved to Cocagne in 1984.

Canadian units advancing in the Liri Valley between the Gustav and Hitler Lines on May 24, 1944. Armand Landry took part in the fighting. LAC / PA 140208

Chapter Eight

"Like a dream"
The Story of Armand Landry

They became friends in England in the summer of 1943 when they joined the Royal 22nd Regiment, the "Van Doos." One was from the Memramcook Valley in southeast New Brunswick, the other from the Republic of Madawaska in the province's northwest. Both had worked in the forest industry. After ten months in combat in Italy, the two inseparables were torn apart by the fortunes of war. At the end of December 1944, they were at the front on the Senio River in northern Italy. All of a sudden, Alban LeBlanc,[32] from Notre-Dame-de-Lourdes, was wounded by shrapnel. Less than forty-eight hours later, his brother in arms, Armand Landry, from Saint-François-de-Madawaska, was captured by the Germans. And so ended their association as combatants.

Even if they were from opposite ends of the province, the two young men had similar experiences. They were both called up for service, but volunteered for overseas before their date. They were both sent to the Voltigeurs de Québec, but they only met after arriving in England.

---

32   The story of Alban LeBlanc is told in the author's *The Forgotten Soldiers* (New Ireland Press, 1990), chap. 5.

That's where they decided to disband the Voltigeurs for reinforcements for other regiments. I met Alban LeBlanc in July 1943 when I arrived with the Royal 22nd. When we left England in September, we didn't know where we were going. They only told us we'd be taking a ship. That's the way things worked. We went to North Africa for training in the mountains. After three months, we were off to Italy. We left between Christmas and New Year's. It took us two and a half days to cross from Africa to Italy. The small ships didn't go very fast. We landed in Naples on New Year's Day morning.

They were on their way to reinforce the Royal 22nd, which had been in combat since July 10, 1943. The regiment had landed in Sicily with 1st Canadian Infantry Division, and on September 3 set foot on the mainland of southern Italy. By December, they had reached Ortona on the Adriatic coast. The fighting decimated their ranks during this long march of more than 500 kilometres.

We took the train in the evening to head to the front. It didn't go very fast in the dark. We were all cramped together in small boxcars, about fifty per car, one on top of the other. We went up to the front in stages. We stayed in Avellino about a week. We spent another week in San Vito before arriving in San Apollinare, where we joined the regiment. The Royal 22nd was resting after the hard fighting at Casa Berardi.[33] We could hear the guns firing when we neared the front. At night, when it was calm, we heard the large cannons shooting some twenty miles away. It aroused our curiosity. Before that, we didn't think the war existed because we hadn't experienced much except for a small bombing raid on our convoy on our way to North Africa. We questioned the veterans, those who had taken part in the Sicilian campaign, to find out what

---

33   Casa Berardi was a large stone farmhouse along a strategic road west of Ortona. Various regiments had tried unsuccessfully to take the position. The Royal 22nd captured the farm in mid-December.

was going on. They didn't dare tell us much because they didn't want to scare us. They said: "Don't be scared guys. It's not as dangerous as it appears." They had to tell us something because we were getting nervous. We were all young men who hadn't known combat.

Landry got his first taste of combat at the beginning of February 1944 with No. 13 Platoon of C Company.

An officer arrived one morning and told us: "We're heading to the front, to relieve another regiment." When we got there, we dug holes, small trenches. Everything was quiet. We were two by two, a new guy like me and one who had combat experience. We did guard duty at night. From time to time, a machine gun would fire some distance away, not too close. We kept our ears open, we were apprehensive. Our first real experience at the front was our patrol against Crecchio [the night of February 8/9]. We hadn't been with the regiment for long and that's where we saw what war was really like. We were scared enough to understand it was dangerous when bullets whizzed by on each side of your head.

We left with about thirty of us. It was a large patrol. They called it a fighting patrol that had to do reconnaissance. It was dark when we left, we couldn't see ten feet ahead of us. We advanced in single file across fields and crossed country roads. They had sent Sergeant Lefebvre and Private Gaudet ahead to give us the signal to start our attack. We walked at least two miles and stopped at the bottom of a hill. The village was perched on the side of the mountain above us. When the sergeant killed the night sentry, Gaudet shot a flare to signal to start the attack. That's when things began, machine guns and mortars firing at the houses, at the windows where the Germans were hiding. They dropped grenades down the hill. Another section, led by Sergeant Gauthier, left to go around the mountain. We stayed there throwing grenades and firing our machine gun. The

Germans did the same but they couldn't hit us because what they threw fell behind a wall which protected us. We spent about half an hour there. Only one man from our group, a guy named Nadeau, was wounded by a bullet in the knee. Sergeant Gauthier also came back later that night with all his men.

Over the next few months, they saw little activity, only a few night patrols and sporadic shelling. What bothered Landry and his companions was the miserable weather.

We weren't comfortable because we had to stay in our trenches. No houses...it was in trenches day and night with only a blanket and a small cape in the middle of winter. It wasn't very warm at times. There was a lot of rain and wet snow. You were numb with cold and your feet were always wet and in the mud. It was quite hard. We had to remain there; it was our duty to stay in those trenches. We went to the rear once in a while, maybe 500 yards, where the trenches were better because they were covered. We did two hours' guard duty, then four hours in the rear trenches. In April, the weather warmed up and we changed front and headed to the Hitler Line. We crossed Italy from one side to the other in trucks. The sun was out and things went well until we hit the Hitler Line. There things were different.

The Canadians joined American and British forces that had been stymied since mid-January in front of Monte Cassino. All efforts to capture the position dominating the road to Rome had ended in failure. The Royal 22nd arrived in front of the German defensive positions in mid-May along with the other two regiments of 3rd Brigade, The Carleton and York and The West Nova Scotia Regiment. The Germans had had months to prepare this sector against a new Allied assault. The Royal 22nd began its advance against the villages of Pontecorvo and Aquino on May 23. For Landry, it was a whole new experience to attack a well-entrenched enemy.

They sent the Carleton and York and the West Novas ahead of us. The Royal 22nd was in reserve. Our regiment went ahead of the others in the afternoon. We had to probe the German line. We stopped. The colonel told us we had to stop because nothing could make it across enemy lines. It was like a thunder and lightning storm. We retreated about 500 yards. They told us to get ready to try to cross the lines the next day. That's where my friend Alban LeBlanc won the Military Medal. We had been together since winter. He found that a rifle wasn't big enough to defend oneself. If he was to be armed, he preferred a Bren gun. That's when I became his partner. I carried the six fifty-round magazines as well as my rifle. It all weighed quite a lot. Some Germans popped up with their hands in the air then ducked down again. We didn't know if they wanted to surrender or what. We advanced until we could see where they were. Two of them were in a machine-gun nest firing on our guys and another rose as if to give up. Alban and I advanced. I was suddenly hit. It was like I had received a blow from a sledgehammer, it hurt! I told Alban I thought I was wounded. He said it couldn't be. I ran my hand but there was nothing. It was probably a ricochet from a piece of rock. I really thought I had been wounded.

The Germans had tried to kill his friend Armand, and Alban LeBlanc was mad. He reacted without hesitating.

That's when Alban cleared out the machine-gun nest. This battle lasted part of the morning. There were many wounded and dead. We advanced with the tanks but we weren't able to penetrate the line. We came back to the rear. In the afternoon, the colonel told us to send a patrol to see where the Carleton and York, which had gone into the line, was. It was like an earthquake there. The lieutenant spoke to an officer of the Carleton and York and we came back to report to Colonel Allard.[34] Allard was the best command-ing officer we ever had. He was a real gentleman, a sincere man. If some guys went out on patrol one evening, he'd send another group the next night. For him, everyone was equal.

By the end of May, the Hitler Line was finally breached and the road to Rome was open, in large part due to the efforts of the Canadians. Most of the men believed they would be the liberators of the Eternal City, but on June 1 the order came to halt the attack when they were at Anagni, less than 50 kilometres from the Italian capital. The Americans under General Mark Clark went ahead of the Canadians and liberated Rome on June 4. For Clark there was no question of the Canadians' entering Rome before his Americans. The Royal 22nd retraced its steps, crossed May's battlefields, and set up camp in Piedimonte d'Alife, about 100 kilometres south. The regiment did not return to combat until early September.

Two events marked the history of the Royal 22nd during this time away from the front. On July 2, the regiment finally entered Rome, and the next day it was received in audience at the Vatican by Pope Pius XII. On the thirty-first, King George VI visited the troops of 1st Canadian Division. The sovereign decorated Canadians whose feats of arms were being rewarded. Armand Landry was certainly very proud to see George VI pin the Military Medal on his friend Alban LeBlanc.

In September, the Van Doos returned to active operations.

We advanced against the Gothic Line at the beginning of September. This operation was nearly as hard as the attack against the Hitler Line. The Gothic Line was heavily fortified. We advanced with the tanks when the terrain allowed it. The men felt safer when there were tanks to support the infantry. We didn't hear much from our air force, we didn't see it very often. I only saw it three times the whole time I was there.

---

34   Lieutenant-Colonel Jean V. Allard took command of the Royal 22nd Regiment on December 18, 1943.

Men of the Royal 22nd Regiment received in audience
by Pope Pius XII at the Vatican, July 1944. Photo LAC / PA-166069

The air force would not have been of much help at the end of December 1944, when the Royal 22nd occupied positions on the south bank of the Senio River in northeast Italy. That is where the Landry-LeBlanc duo was torn apart.

I was taken prisoner on December 27 or 28. Alban was wounded a day or two before. He had shrapnel in his legs. He was about twenty feet from me when hit. It was sunset when he came to tell me he was leaving because of his wound. We were along the Senio, between Bagnacavallo and Lugo, when I was captured. We were two sections dug in behind a dike on one side of a canal. The Germans were on the other side. They wanted to send flamethrowers to the top of the hill to fire at the Germans. They told us to carry on digging to keep the Germans busy. We dug our holes twenty-five feet apart and fired machine guns and rifles. The river wasn't very wide, not more than a hundred feet. We were so close to the Germans we could hear them talk. We fired until three or four in the morning. We began to run out of ammunition. The rest of the company was in trenches about a thousand feet behind us. We fired less often, only a shot once in a while to keep the Germans busy. Our guys never came with their flamethrowers on Bren carriers.

Dawn was just breaking when the Germans crossed the river without us seeing them because we were on the reverse side of the dike. They climbed up, about ten of them with big submachine guns. They said: *"Raus!"* — get up. They made us cross the river and marched us a mile under guard. We were eight. We climbed aboard small Volkswagens to go to a little camp where they regrouped their prisoners.

Alban LeBlanc recovered from his wound and returned to the front. For Armand Landry, the fighting was over. He was on his way to a POW camp in Germany.

We spent a week and a half in that little camp. From there, we boarded freight cars to be taken to Germany. The trip wasn't very nice. We were fifty in our boxcar. We were not all Canadians. There were black Americans, Greeks, and all those Germans had picked up on the battlefield. When they had enough prisoners to fill seven or eight boxcars, they sent us to Germany. They gave us a ration in the morning: two slices of bread and salami. We had to wait until the next morning to get anything else to eat. The guards opened the doors, gave us our ration, and shut them again. We couldn't get out. We didn't get a drop of water for four days and nights because the Royal Air Force had bombed a bridge to the north in the Alps. The Germans used to write POW on the cars full of prisoners. They transported tanks and cannons for repair in Germany on the same train. They just had enough time to stop the train before getting to the bridge. They backed it up in a tunnel for four days and nights while they repaired the bridge.

The toilet was a wooden box. The guys did their business in it. It smelled bad after a while. It overflowed and ran all over the floor. We had to sleep on the floor on piss-soaked straw. On the fourth day, they finally brought us water. We were eager to get to the other end. The train left. It took us another day to reach Moosburg in Germany. We were happy to get off the train. We had long beards and hadn't eaten or slept much. The camp wasn't far from the station. There was snow, it wasn't warm in January. Some of the guys were weak and fell. We picked them up and dragged them to the camp.

When Landry arrived at *Stalag* VIIa in mid-January 1945, the camp was overflowing because of the large number of prisoners arriving from Italy and Belgium.[35]

It was so well guarded that it was nearly impossible to escape. There were dogs, eighteen-foot fences with three rows of barbed wire, mines, and guard towers. As soon as we got to camp, they confiscated our leather vests and took pictures for our identity cards. They then sent us to barracks with other Canadians who had been captured before. There were also Americans, British, Greeks, French, and Russians. Each group had its own barrack. There must have been at least twenty thousand men. There were three barracks for Canadians. Officers had their own, but in each barrack there was an officer in charge of the group. If someone was sick, he reported it. We were between seventy-five and one hundred per barrack. There were three-tiered bunks and we had a thin, straw-filled mattress. We only had one small blanket.

---

35   The camp population increased sharply with the arrival of Americans captured during the Battle of the Bulge in Belgium at the end of December 1944.

It wasn't warm in winter. There was little coal and firewood because, at that time, the Germans were severely rationed. They didn't have enough for themselves and couldn't give any to prisoners.

It was the same thing with food and cigarettes. What helped a little were the Red Cross parcels we got from time to time. They came from Canada and the United States. We had to share one among three guys. Inside were four packs of cigarettes, small tins of meat, coffee, tea, and milk. It wasn't much but it helped. The guys in our barracks got to know each other well after a time. When we got a parcel, we gave it to one man to share it with the guys next to him or in the same row of beds. If you didn't like something in it, you could trade for something else. We usually got a parcel every week or two but after a while they only arrived every three weeks. They became scarcer near the end because the Germans kept them for themselves. They didn't tell us how many Red Cross parcels arrived at the camp. They were so badly rationed, they had to eat too. For example, every German soldier got two cigarettes a day. In the Red Cross parcels, there were four packs…Camels, Lucky Strike, and Chesterfield. I often traded cigarettes for bread with the Germans. The bread was nearly black and some said it contained sawdust. The trading was mostly at night. Those who guarded us during the day had nothing to exchange. We weren't very well fed even if we had to work every day except Sunday. We worked on the rail lines in Munich [forty kilometres south], at Landshut [twenty kilometres north], and elsewhere. After a while, we knew the names of all the train stations to Munich and announced them when we got there. Our guards found that funny.

Like fellow prisoner Alcide Gallant, Landry "passed by Dachau two or three times on our way to Munich but we didn't know what was going on there. The guards told us nothing and we didn't ask questions. We knew it was a camp because of the barbed wire."

Munich railyard, which prisoners from *Stalag* VIIa were sent to repair after its bombing by the Americans. Alamy stock photo ID TA-2AGX

The Allies bombed Munich and Landshut. The next day, the Germans put us on a train and took us to repair the damages. We were six to eight prisoners for one guard. We weren't allowed to speak with civilians and they didn't have the right to talk to us. As soon as a civilian approached, the guards shooed him away. We saw bombers drop their loads a couple of times but they weren't near us. Every day, British and American planes flew right over us at maybe one hundred feet. They saw prisoners working in different areas. They were on their way to bomb war plants farther on. They bombed train stations at night.

Stalag VIIa held prisoners from most of the Allied countries, but not all were treated equally.

Our guards treated us quite well. I can't say they were hard with us. They didn't push us to work but we had to hustle just the same. Many of them loved to yell but I can't say our guards were bad guys. The Russians in camp suffered a lot. They had many wounded, men missing an arm or fingers, but they had no medicine. It was like the Germans didn't want to treat the wounded. The Russians didn't have any doctors to take care of them and they had to bandage themselves. I felt sorry; nobody was taking care of them. Some died after a while because they became infected. They also had less rations than us. The Germans were against the Russians. Us, we had our doctors who had been captured. When you said "*Kanadier*" or "*Amerikaner*," you were treated better.

Landry spent only four months in Moosburg. When he arrived, German morale was already on the wane and most recognized that the end was near.

The Germans felt defeated during the last months of the war and told us so. That's why they were less harsh on the prisoners. They had also moderated their propaganda. Some spoke very good French or English. We questioned them. Many said they were defeated but others still didn't believe it. Some even said they were going to come to grab land in Canada.

The German guards who still believed in Germany's final victory had to confront the reality of defeat when the order came to evacuate part of the camp. For Landry, it was the sign that liberation was inevitable.

Around mid-April, they came to tell us we were leaving. We were about ten thousand, to whom they each gave a box of rations before going. We took to the road. We didn't know where we were going. When we asked the guards, they didn't know either. If I remember well, we marched for nine days. We walked from morning until night. We stopped in small villages at night. We slept in barns and sheds. I think we were heading north towards Berlin. Planes flew right over us every day. They flew very low and wiggled their wings. They knew that a group like ours on the road weren't German troops but prisoners of war. On the evening of the ninth day, we entered the village of Ettlingen [near Karlsruhe and the border with France].

We again slept in sheds because we didn't have the right to enter houses and take beds from civilians. The guards were there to make sure we didn't escape or bother civilians. A short time after we stopped, a German officer who spoke French arrived. He said: "Tonight, we sleep here. Tomorrow morning, at ten o'clock, American tanks will be here in the village. At ten o'clock exactly." He must have known what he was talking about. He told us that they, the Germans, were leaving. The guards warned us not to leave the village because the Americans knew where we were and that there were still German troops everywhere. Our guards said: "Good night and good luck!" then left.

Next morning, at exactly ten o'clock, American tanks entered the village. The guys in the tanks threw us cartons of cigarettes and chocolate bars. They told us to stay put because the kitchens, the shower trucks, and clothes were coming behind them. About an hour later, they began to arrive: American trucks, jeeps, and ambulances. They were all mixed in among the tanks... it was like an earthquake. They began by having us take showers and gave us new clothes. They fed us and gave us more cigarettes. They told us to stay where we were because they had to separate everyone. Every Canadian got an identity card with the name of his regiment and other details. Everyone was separated by nationality: Canadians together, Americans on one side, Russians on the other, and so on.

The weather was nasty; it was rainy and foggy. They told us we would be taken to France as soon as the weather cleared. We stayed in Ettlingen for a week. We were about 150, the others were in villages in front or behind us. They came to get us with Buffalos [amphibious vehicles] because there were not enough trucks to transport all of us. They drove us to an airfield. When we got to the airfield, I saw a nice German air force officer's cap laying on the ground. It was brand new. I picked it up and put it on my head. I thought they might take it from me but managed to keep it. I brought it back to Canada. We boarded Douglas DC-3s. They flew us to France.... When we got off the plane, they told us the war had just ended.

Juvincourt-et-Damary, where they landed, is a village about twenty kilometres north of Reims. The French had built a military airfield there before the war, and the Germans used it after the fall of France in June 1940. Captured by the Americans in September 1944, it became an important centre for the repatriation of prisoners of war by the RAF at the end of hostilities.

We slept in Juvincourt that evening, and the next morning we climbed aboard Lancaster bombers heading for England. We were about twenty per plane, jammed against one another. Those planes weren't designed to transport men. I told myself that it wouldn't be long before I was back home in Canada.

Landry believed he would see his native Madawaska in a few weeks, but his hope of heading home was put on hold by the Canadian military's system for the repatriation of combatants.

They began by returning to Canada the first who had crossed overseas in 1939. Those who went over in 1940, 1941, and 1942 all went home before me. I was unable to rejoin my regiment because I had been a prisoner. I was in another category, and I stayed in England from May 1945 until March 1946. I had tried to rejoin my unit by all imaginable means, but was unable. I had to wait for my turn to come home because I had only crossed in 1943. My friend Alban LeBlanc had made it home and wrote to me in England.

Landry finally got back to Canada in March 1946 and was demobilized a month later. His return to civilian life failed to erase the memory of his experiences on the battlefield, but he did not talk about them, not even to Élianne Martin, who became his wife in January 1948. She often saw him absorbed in thought but did not say anything. It was only two and a half years after their marriage that he finally opened up and his memories spilled out.

What happened on the front and my capture by the Germans was a difficult and complicated adventure but I never regretted it. You always think of what happened but it's like in a dream. Some can never forget. Even if I had told my story, people wouldn't have believed it. They would have said I was a liar. I wanted to keep it inside. It's hard, people not believing you when you're telling the truth. It's nearly unbelievable because you can't tell all that happened on the battlefield. People think it's impossible. It's twice as bad as what we can see in war movies. When you see friends with bullets in their knees, their shoulders, or their stomach and you hear them yelling "Come help me!" it's hard on morale. You know you can be hit any time. How many fell next to us, their head split wide open or their body riddled by machine-gun bullets. I hear them calling out: "Come help me. Mother, father...I'm going to die!"

Half a century after the war, Armand Landry still heard them. He went back to work for Fraser Pulp and Paper. He did forestry camp maintenance for more than thirty-six years until his retirement in 1983. He and his wife Élianne had three children and lived in Iroquois, near Edmundston.

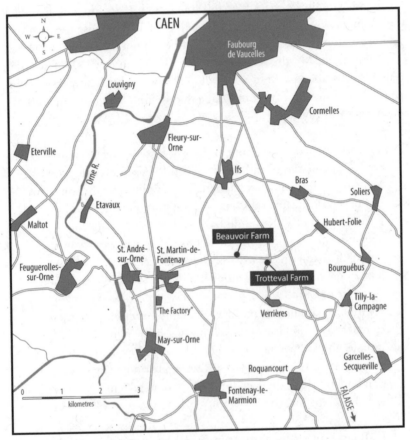

Beauvoir and Trotteval farms in Normandy, where Les Fusiliers
Mont-Royal engaged the Germans between July 20 and July 22, 1944.

Ronald Cormier / Mike Bechthold

Chapter Nine

The Death March
The Story of Léo Vienneau

At 12:42 p.m. on July 20, 1944, an explosion reverberated through Adolf Hitler's headquarters in the Rastenburg Forest in East Prussia. Hitler was slightly injured and a few officers from his general staff were killed. Hitler had called his advisors to his eastern headquarters to discuss the military situation on the Eastern Front and in Normandy. The explosion of a time-delayed bomb hidden in an attaché case left under the conference room table by Colonel Claus von Stauffenberg was part of a plot to rid Germany of Hitler and the Nazis. The conspirators hoped to take power and negotiate the end of hostilities with the Allies on the Western Front. The plot failed.

As Hitler and his entourage recovered from the shock of the explosion, 2nd Canadian Infantry Division launched attacks on objectives in Normandy, more than 1,500 kilometres from Rastenburg. Among the units that left their start line at 1500 hours was a regiment from Montreal, Les Fusiliers Mont-Royal. Their objective was Verrières, a village at the top of a hill south of Caen, on the main road to Falaise. The regiment was undertaking its first major operation since arriving in Normandy in early July, but this was not its first encounter with the Germans. The battalion had suffered heavy losses two years earlier during the raid on Dieppe on August 19, 1942.[36]

The regiment was rebuilt after Dieppe, and most of the men advancing toward Verrières on July 20 had never seen action. Among them was Léo Vienneau from Caraquet Island (Pokesudie Island), New Brunswick, a corporal with B Company. For Vienneau, the route between his native island and his first encounter with the enemy had been long. "I volunteered. One of my older brothers was already in the army. On the island, there was no work. Fishing was not doing great and I decided to enlist [on January 22, 1942]. I was twenty-one."

After his basic training in Fredericton and Edmundston, Vienneau found himself in North Bay, Ontario, where he learned skills other than the handling of weapons.

I didn't know how to read or write. They took soldiers to school. We went to class for fifteen or twenty minutes a day between drill periods. I learned to sign my name and to write a few words. One of my nephews from Bathurst was with me. He knew how to read and write. One day, he said to me: "You're going to write a letter to your girlfriend." I wrote two pages which he corrected.

After North Bay, Vienneau was off to Valcartier, Quebec, for advanced training, then on to Debert, Nova Scotia, before leaving for overseas on the *Queen Elizabeth* in December 1942. He arrived in Scotland on Christmas Eve.

Vienneau and his regiment did not take part in the Normandy landings on June 6, 1944, but they and the other regiments of 2nd Canadian Infantry Division were called upon for the second phase of the battle after the capture of Caen. Les Fusiliers Mont-Royal set foot on French soil for a second time on July 7. Their first assignment, capturing the village of Verrières, was part of Operation Atlantic.

---

36   Only 125 of the 548 officers and men of Les Fusiliers Mont-Royal who took part in the raid returned to England after the operation. The regiment suffered 119 dead and more than 150 wounded; another 344 became prisoners of war.

The riflemen of Les Fusiliers Mont-Royal began their attack after having marched all night and without eating since the previous evening. Halfway between their start line and Verrières were two farms named Beauvoir and Trotteval. B Company advanced toward Beauvoir farm, and everything seemed to be going smoothly until they reached it. Suddenly, German troops hidden nearby appeared. "I was a corporal and I was in charge of a section of eight men. My section was leading B Company. My Bren gunner was in front. The Germans were shooting at us. We dug trenches and laid down in them. We didn't have a choice." Although most of the soldiers had no combat experience, they resisted fierce counter-attacks by the German 272nd Division supported by tanks from 1st Panzer Division SS. The men of Les Fusiliers Mont-Royal fought valiantly, but most quickly faced reality.

It rained for two days. Our trenches filled with water. Our rifles didn't work any longer, they were jammed. It didn't really matter because we ran out of ammunition. I told my men that we had to try to get reinforcements and send someone to find the major farther back. I sent one of my guys, Joseph Doiron from Caraquet, to see if the major could tell us what to do. We didn't know what to do because our phone line and our radio weren't working. Doiron left but he never returned. He was wounded while making his way to the rear.

When I saw that he wasn't coming back, I told myself that I had to find men. The officer was nearby. I went to see him but he didn't have any orders to give. He couldn't get munitions from the rear either and help us. He told me to do what we wanted. I went back and told my men. I could see the Germans firing as they came towards us. We were in a wheat field near the farm. I could see the ears of wheat being mown down. I asked my men what they thought we should do. They answered that I was in charge of the section. I asked if they were going to do like me. I had never thought of becoming a prisoner. The idea came to me just like that. I told them to drop all their weapons because we were going to surrender. Anyway, we didn't have any ammunition, nothing to defend ourselves with. We couldn't even remove the bayonet from our rifle! After two days of rain, it was rusted tight to the gun. Other sections also gave up when we did [around 3:00 p.m.].

The men of B Company resisted to the limits of their endurance an enemy superior in numbers and weapons. The regiment, mainly B and C Companies, lost 150 officers and men between July 20 and 22. For Corporal Vienneau, it was the beginning of a new ordeal as a prisoner of war.

The Germans took the officers and NCOs [non-commissioned officers] to try to make them talk. They took me because I had been the first one out. They wanted to make me talk. They asked where I had landed in France and the name of my regiment. During training we had been taught not to talk. I gave them my name and number, G 23633, but that wasn't what they wanted. They kept me for about an hour before handing me over to another officer. This one took out his revolver and put in on the side of the table. He began talking quietly in French. He asked where I had landed. I gave him my name and number. He said that if I didn't want to talk, it was a game that two could play. From time to time, he took the revolver in his hand and set it down on the table again. He kept me there for about an hour before telling me I could join my friends.

The Germans took me to a small guard house, no bigger than a refrigerator. They locked me inside. I couldn't even sit and had to crouch down. I spent about three hours there in the July heat. When they opened the door, I was squashed down at the bottom of the shed. They grabbed me by the scruff of the neck and pulled me out. I was then led to a cellar. The Germans were getting ready to go out on an attack. They were about thirty. I leaned back against a wall near the door. Every time a German went out, he either slapped my face or gave me a kick in the rear. I couldn't move because of the guard with his rifle. I was in a hurry to see the last one leave. They were SS troops. They took me out and made me stand with my face against a wall with my hands in the air. They put a revolver in my back and started questioning me again. I spent five hours facing the wall with my hands in the air. It was hard and tiring. If I happened to lower my hands, they stuck me in the back with a gun. At the end, I couldn't answer, I couldn't hear.... I was burnt out. I fainted when they told me to lower my hands. They woke me and took me to another building where there were officers. They were celebrating, they were laughing. They asked my name. I answered: "Léo Vienneau, G 23633." They offered me a cigarette. I didn't say anything. One of them said: "What, you don't smoke?" After that they brought out a glass and a bottle of beer. They offered me some but I didn't reply.

They allowed me to sleep for a while at night. The next day, they began the same routine. They questioned me all day. I only told them my name and number. They kept me for two days in that building. They finally said they were sending me to find my chums who were nearby in the basements of houses. All this questioning made me mad because they knew very well where I had landed.

Every captured soldier had the duty to try to escape if the opportunity arose. After two days of questioning, Vienneau had had enough of German hospitality.

I tried to escape with other guys before we got to the train taking us to the POW camp. A Polish soldier had indicated the British were near. Seven of us, guys from Montreal and Saint John, tried to make our escape. We were walking in a field full of small trees and bushes. We walked by anti-aircraft projectors and threw ourselves on the ground. The Germans found us. They gave us a going over: kicks to the rear end and a whipping. They escorted us to the train. Nobody escaped.

The train journey from Normandy to the POW camp was but a foretaste of the treatment Vienneau would endure at the hands of the enemy.

They put us in boxcars to take us to Germany. All of us who had been captured were locked in for five days. There were British with us. The train was full. We had to take turns sitting down. We didn't have anything to drink or eat. When we passed by streams at night, a sort of frost formed on the head of the nails in the boxcars. We licked it up to drink. We got to Germany after five days. They stopped the train next to a stream and told us we could get out to get a drink. We had a hard time drinking because we had to use our hands. Some were so weak that they passed out. It took some time for us to regain our senses. All of a sudden a farmer came with a drum of milk. That saved us. We got back on the train, which arrived at *Stalag* VIIIb during the night.

Upper Silesia, where *Stalag* VIIIb was located, was a part of old Prussia rich in coal, an essential resource for the German war effort. The camp resembled all others. It was surrounded by fences and barbed wire, with towers where guards armed with machine guns saw to it that prisoners did not escape. Thousands of POWs were already in the camp when Vienneau arrived. Among the few hundred Canadian prisoners were men from Les Fusiliers Mont-Royal captured two years earlier at Dieppe. These early detainees had already adapted to the harsh living conditions. Vienneau, prisoner number 83113, had to learn to do the same.

We were at least fifty per barrack. The beds were set up one over the other the whole length of the building. I was sent to work in a coal mine a week after I got to the camp. I worked there for about six months. It wasn't far from camp. They took us by truck. We went down the mine at six in the evening and came back up at six in the morning. We worked twelve hours. I did my work. Everyone had a job to do at night. There was a shaft about four feet wide and eight feet high which led down. The Germans brought down the coal. Our job was to stack bricks against the wall and fill in the gaps with coal dust. If it took all night to do it, you stayed in the hole. If it only took you an hour, you still stayed there but you did nothing for the rest of the night. I was still in pretty good shape in the beginning and hurried to finish the job. Sometimes I'd be done in two and a half or three hours. It never took me more than three and a half hours. I was then told I could sit down. The other guys asked me: "Why do you work so fast? You must like working for the Germans." I answered that I didn't like it but that it was easier working when I still had my bowl of soup in me.

Raoul LeBouthillier, a guy from Bas-Caraquet, was there with me. I told him it wasn't worth our while to dig in our heels because we were prisoners. Some stubbornly refused to work. They stayed in the mine up to three days without being allowed out. There were all sorts of races: British, Russians, Poles, Ukrainians, and others. The Germans gave us a large bowl of cow beets. We ate it but the British threw it away. When the Germans saw this, they cut our ration to one cup. There were not too many beets in it, it was only juice. We got a cup when we went down the mine in the evening and one when we came up in the morning. We got a parcel of food every fifteen days after the Red Cross traced us. It contained a can of peas and one of meat, a chocolate bar, a pack of cigarettes, and biscuits. It was enough for a meal for one man. There was no beverage so we drank the juice from the can of peas. We could have eaten everything at once but had to make it last as long as possible. In the morning, we ate a biscuit with our cup of soup. It was the same in the evening. A couple of months after my arrival, the Germans decided to give us potatoes. We got only one a week.

Prisoners of war at *Stalag* VIIIb in Lamsdorf, Germany,
brewing tea outdoors. Australian War Memorial / P10548005

I fell ill at work. I was exhausted and had a fever. They took
me to see a doctor. It was in the fall. They admitted me to hospital. I had diphtheria. I spent three days in hospital. As soon as I
returned to camp, they sent me back to work in the mine. I can't
say that the guards were hard on me. The Germans who worked
in the mine were older, between fifty and seventy.

On January 17, 1945, Warsaw was liberated. Farther south, the fighting
on the Eastern Front approached Upper Silesia while Vienneau worked
in the mine. In the face of this threat, German authorities decided to
evacuate the camp rather than allowing the Russians to liberate it. Thus
began a death march that covered hundreds of kilometres through all
regions of Germany.

We marched from the middle of January to the end of April. They forced us to march from the *Stalag* in eastern Germany until we were freed by the Americans. It was winter and sometimes quite cold. It snowed one night in northern Germany. Two or three inches of snow fell and we slept outside. I froze a toe that night and it became infected. We walked all the time. We stopped on the side of the road every five or six hours when there wasn't too much traffic. We only slept eight nights in barns. There, the lice devoured us. They gave us a cup of soup when we stopped at night. That was our ration. Even if you wanted more, that was all we got. The cup of soup was enough because our stomachs had shrunk. The hunger went away but an hour or two later you were hungry again. I spent the whole march with a guy from Montreal, a good guy, a tall dark fellow. We told ourselves that we'd eat a delicious pie or a piece of steak when we got home and we burst out laughing. We dreamt of eating. The Red Cross was following us and brought us a package every fifteen days.

Despite the arrival of Red Cross parcels once in a while, hunger dominated the thoughts of the exhausted prisoners. Hunger pushed some to commit acts they never would have dreamt of in other circumstances. Vienneau was the victim of such desperation.

One time we spent the night in a barn. We had received our Red Cross parcel earlier in the day. There were packs of cigarettes in it, Sweet Caporal. There were a few good guys amongst the guards. One of them saw the packs of cigarettes and called me over to the fence. He spoke French. He said he'd give me a loaf of bread, black bread, if I gave him a pack of cigarettes. I went to get them and he gave me the bread which I hid on my person. When I returned to the barn, I hid it in the straw and covered it with my blanket. I was with Raoul LeBouthillier. I said to myself we'd be having a nice lunch later. Some Irishmen had seen me hiding it. I went out of the barn and one of them stole my bread. When I got

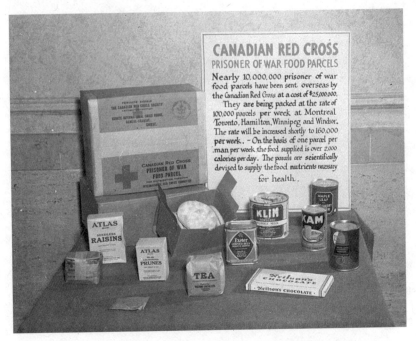

The typical Canadian Red Cross parcel contained 2,000 calories
for one man for a week. LAC / PA-065176

back, guys who had seen him told me a tall red-headed guy had
taken it. I had lost everything: the bread and the cigarettes.

The lack of food, rest, medical care, and the cold quickly led to
exhaustion among the prisoners during the three months of this never-
ending march. It was march or die.

Some guys fell down and couldn't get up. The guards shot them.
Raoul LeBouthillier fell ill during the march. He only weighed
about sixty pounds. My friend from Montreal was quite strong.
I told him my friend LeBouthillier would die if we didn't carry
him. We carried him on our backs for four days. We weren't that
strong ourselves but we took turns. We put him on our backs and

held his hands hanging around our neck. That's how we carried him. If we had left him there, the Germans would have shot him. The day before our liberation, we lost sight of Raoul. We just couldn't carry him any longer. We told ourselves he was dead, that the Germans had killed him.

By the second week of April 1945, the war was coming to an end in Europe. The Americans, British, and Canadians captured thousands of prisoners in western Germany while the Russian army crushed the last pockets of resistance in Berlin. The Allied victory meant liberation for Vienneau and the thirty thousand or so men in the POW column extending over tens of kilometres.

We saw a plane fly over in the morning. We also met a Pole who worked on a farm. He told us not to worry because we would be liberated during the day. About an hour before being freed, the German guards came to find us. They had us sit down and told us they were "*kaput,*" that they were finished. They knew the Americans were coming. They gave us their rifles. I remember that it was about three o'clock when we saw the Americans arrive. There was a big tank and soldiers. They surrounded us. We didn't have anything, no clothes, absolutely nothing. We only had our POW uniforms with KG, for *Kriegie* [short for *Kriegsgefangener*, prisoner of war] written on the back when the Americans freed us. We didn't have anything on our feet because our army boots were all worn out. We were dirty.

The Americans brought in a boxcar with showers in it. They disinfected us with a powder [probably DDT]. It was sickening; we walked on lice! It took two days to wash everybody. They gave us new clothes because we didn't have anything left to wear. We spent eight days there. They prepared barns and other buildings for us to sleep in. The Americans fed us, but we were sick when we ate because our stomachs couldn't take the food. At the end of the eight days, they found an airfield and flew us to France.

I spent fifteen days in hospital somewhere in France. From there they flew us to England, where I spent a month in hospital. I weighed eighty pounds when I was liberated. I was only skin and bones. In two months, I was up to 160 pounds. I only weighed 121 or 122 pounds when I was captured.

Thoughts of lost friends were fresh in Vienneau's memory when he arrived at the hospital in England. He was in for quite a surprise: "Raoul LeBouthillier was there when I got to England. The Germans had taken him to hospital. They had stopped shooting prisoners during the final days. From Germany, Raoul had been taken to England. When I saw him in the hospital bed, I told him I thought he was dead. He also believed I was dead. We enlisted at the same time and came back to Canada together."

Peace reigned in Europe when Corporal Vienneau left hospital in England after his convalescence, but the war against Japan still raged in the Pacific. "I loved the army. I didn't want to come back to Canada; I wanted to go to Japan. When I talked to the commanding officer, he told me to go home, that I had done my part. Many of us were like that." Even if Vienneau wanted to take part in a war that, for all intents and purposes, had escaped him because of his capture after only a few days in combat, his health did not allow him to go to Japan. He was still suffering from the effects of the death march. "I spent about fifteen days in hospital at the base in Fredericton after I came back to Canada. My legs were sore, I suffered from rheumatism. I was then sent as an instructor to train new recruits. I left the army on August 15, 1945."

When a man goes off to war, he leaves behind parents, brothers, and sisters. His family knows there is the possibility he will not return, but are hopeful that he will make it through safe and sound. We can easily imagine the concerns of Vienneau's parents in the summer of 1944 when they learned that he was missing in action. "I was reported missing. It was at least two months before my mother learned I was a prisoner of war." His family was bereaved shortly before his capture. Corporal Vienneau had just arrived at the front when he learned the sad news. "I was in my trench one evening when the sergeant major came over with another guy. It was Joseph Doiron from Caraquet. He was coming to join my section. He told me my eldest brother had passed away since I had crossed overseas."

Léo Vienneau considered himself lucky to have survived the death march, which lasted more than three months. The memory of those events was etched in his mind, and his health suffered ever after from the terrible conditions of the march. Vienneau went back to fishing when he returned home. He worked in the offshore fishery for three years and another seventeen fishing for lobster. He later worked at a fish-processing plant in Caraquet. In 1946, he married Angéline Gionet; they lived in Bas-Caraquet and had eight children.

Léo Pitre (left) from Jacquet River, New Brunswick, and Léo Johnson
(right) from Bathurst on August 15, 1945. According to Pitre,
"This photo was taken by a young Japanese woman the day after
my liberation. It was the first time I put on my uniform
since my capture in Hong Kong." Collection of Léo Pitre

Chapter Ten

"A beating every day"
The Story of Léo Pitre

Half a world separates New Brunswick from the former British colony of Hong Kong. It is hard to imagine Acadians leaving their homeland to fight in Southeast Asia during the Second World War. It is, however, the case that dozens of young Acadians made that fateful trip at the end of 1941. Two Canadian regiments, The Royal Rifles of Canada and The Winnipeg Grenadiers, sent by the Mackenzie King government, counted many Acadians in their ranks. Among the Royal Rifles was a young man from Jacquet River.

Léo Pitre was twenty years old when he volunteered for the army on October 16, 1940. "I was working in the woods at the time. All my friends from Jacquet River had joined the army. There was nothing else to do but enlist. I joined the Royal Rifles,[37] an English regiment from Quebec City. As soon as the regiment was mobilized, it was transferred to the camp in Sussex. That's where I joined it." His regiment was posted to Newfoundland in December 1940. After nine months, it came back to Canada and eventually returned to Quebec City in August 1941.

At about the same time, the commanding officer of British forces in China responsible for the garrison at Hong Kong was replaced and called

---

37   The Royal Rifles actively recruited on the Gaspé Peninsula and in northern New Brunswick.

Members of The Royal Rifles of Canada prepare to leave Valcartier, Quebec, for Hong Kong, October 1941. LAC / PA-116794

back to Britain. Major-General Arthur Edward Grasset, a senior officer of Canadian origin, travelled through Canada on his way to London. He stopped in Ottawa to see his old colleague from the Royal Military College, Lieutenant-General Harry Crerar, Canada's Chief of the General Staff. Arriving in London, Grasset pleaded with his superiors to reinforce the Hong Kong garrison. Prime Minister Winston Churchill, who was cool to the idea that it was possible to defend the colony against an eventual Japanese attack, finally rallied to Grasset's position. Grasset told his superiors that Canada might be willing to send one or two battalions to reinforce the colony. On September 19, 1941, the Canadian government received a request[38] along those lines from Britain, which urgently needed more troops in Hong Kong. The war cabinet consulted Crerar, who advised that "the Canadian Army should take this on."[39]

---

38 Telegram "Most Secret" from the Secretary of State for Dominion Affairs to the Government of Canada, September 19, 1941.
39 Crerar denied having told Grasset that Canada might be willing to send troops, but he admitted having discussed the Hong Kong situation with him.

The Royal Rifles and The Winnipeg Grenadiers were both Class C units—garrison troops. The Royal Rifles had served in Newfoundland and the Grenadiers in Bermuda and Jamaica. The two battalions, untrained for combat, left Vancouver on the Australian liner *Awatea* on October 27, 1941. The 1,975 men under the command of Brigadier John K. Lawson only learned a few days after sailing that Force C was heading to Hong Kong. According to Pitre, "It took twenty-two days to reach Hong Kong. From Vancouver, we stopped in Hawaii. We arrived in Hong Kong in mid-November [on the sixteenth]."

War in the Pacific had not yet broken out when they disembarked but the political climate was extremely tense. The Japanese occupied a large part of China, but Western countries underestimated the strength of the Japanese army because they believed it incapable of measuring up on the battlefield. Three weeks after Pitre's arrival, events in Hong Kong took a dramatic turn.

We had only been there a few days when Japan attacked Pearl Harbor, in Hawaii. The first Japanese attacks began in the afternoon. Many of us had gone to see a movie. An hour later, the sergeant came in and told us to return to camp [Sham Shui Po] because the Japanese had declared war and started bombing. We returned to camp and picked up our equipment. We marched twelve miles to take the ferry to cross to the island [Hong Kong Island].[40] We hadn't been gone more than half an hour before the Japanese bombed it.

On December 11, the fourteen thousand Canadian, Scottish, and Indian defenders evacuated the New Territories and concentrated in defensive positions on Hong Kong Island. A week later, Japanese forces landed on the island and captured more than half of it over the next twenty-four hours. The defenders were in an untenable situation. Nobody could reinforce them. They were left to their fate.

---

40   Sham Shui Po camp was in Kowloon, on the mainland.

The fighting was hard because we had nothing to fight with, only fifty rounds of ammunition and two or three grenades each. I only drank a small can of Carnation milk and ate three or four biscuits and two slices of raw bacon during the sixteen days I was in combat. That's all I had to eat in sixteen days. It was impossible to fight on an empty stomach. The fighting was hard. There were ten Japanese for every one of us. We only had our bayonets left to fight with after we ran out of ammunition. It didn't make sense to fight because there were too many Japanese. They were good fighters; they had been training since the age of five or six. A lot of men from my company [B Company] were killed.[41] My officer was killed after three or four days. Three other officers died when they stepped on a mine.

After seventeen days of fighting against an adversary largely superior in numbers and arms, Hong Kong's military commander, Major-General Christopher Maltby, decided to capitulate. For Pitre, the war ended on December 25.

Christmas Eve, around ten o'clock, our officer told us: "It's every man for himself. We don't have any ammunition. Fend for yourself!" I'll never forget that. Christmas Night, we were at Stanley Mound, which we called Stanley Fort. My friend and I were at the front, among boulders, when the sergeant came to tell us to make our way to camp, that the war was over. All of a sudden, the lights came on all over the place. We went to the camp and lay all our rifles in a pile on the ground.

It was only twenty-four hours later that Pitre and nearly 1,700 other Canadian soldiers began to understand what fate awaited them at the hands of the Japanese.

---

41   Canadians suffered 290 fatal casualties in Hong Kong.

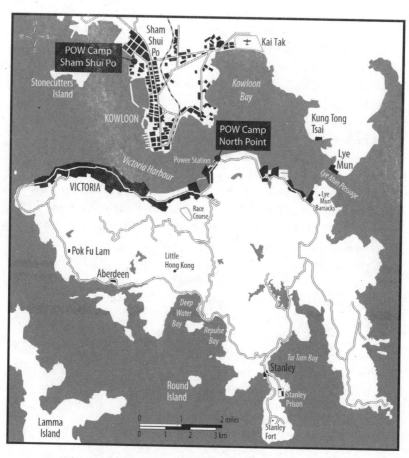

After capturing the New Territories, the Japanese landed on
Hong Kong Island, where the Allies surrendered on December 25, 1941.
Two POW camps were set up: North Point on the island and
Sham Shui Po in Kowloon. Ronald Cormier / Mike Bechthold

The Japanese arrived at camp at midnight the next day. They began by taking all our munitions and clothes. They took everything we had. They even pulled gold teeth from the mouths of some men. One guy had a nice large ring. When they couldn't pull it off his finger, they cut off his finger to get it. Nothing bothered them. They made us get undressed. We were buck naked. We stood like that from midnight until four o'clock in the afternoon. They took all we had: clothes, watches, rings, everything. When we saw that the Japanese were starting to mistreat us, it came to us we would not survive. We had been told that the Japanese took no prisoners, that they killed them right away. That's what they did to many of our medical staff. They killed seven. They tied them to fence posts and bayoneted them. One of the Japanese officers had been badly wounded. They came to get a doctor and told him that they would let us live if he saved their officer's life. He saved his life and that's probably what saved us. It didn't stop them from killing others later. They, at least, were not abused later in the camps. They marched us twelve miles to North Point,[42] which became our first prisoner of war camp. The North Point camp looked like a barn, a pigsty. We slept on blankets outside on the pavement.

When Pitre and the others arrived at North Point a few days after Christmas, they were in relatively good shape despite the hardships they had endured in the battle. Their morale was still good enough for them to think of escaping.

We were about a dozen getting ready to escape. The colonel said he wouldn't stop us because it was our duty. The Japanese had divided us into groups of ten and had put a man in charge of each group. They told us they'd kill the ten if one of them escaped. It wasn't worth the risk to try. Two men escaped. The Japanese

---

42   North Point was an old Chinese refugee camp located on the north side of Hong Kong Island.

caught one and killed him. The other managed to cross China and reach Russia. From there, he was sent back to Canada.

Few tried to escape from North Point and even fewer survived their attempts. In most cases, the Japanese executed them as soon as they were recaptured. The cruelty shown to POWs stemmed from the warrior philosophy instilled in Japanese soldiers since their youth. The warrior code of conduct said that every soldier must fight to the death for his Emperor. A soldier who was captured by the enemy lost honour and respect. It is through this optic that one has to view the attitude of the Japanese toward their prisoners. Pitre and his compatriots became slaves of the Empire of the Rising Sun. Their martyrdom began at North Point.

I can't say we really had anything to eat. We only got rice, grass, leaves, and pieces of potatoes. We ate more worms than anything else. The rice was often rotten or mouldy. For breakfast, we were given a small rice ration. For dinner, we got a small potato or half a large one. For supper, it was hot water with nothing in it. The only time we got bread was when we went down to the docks to clean the buildings where they loaded flour. We picked up the flour which had fallen from torn bags. There was sand, ants, fleas, and other stuff in it. We took it back to camp and cooked it with water. It was as hard as wood.

The Japanese had fixed the daily ration for each prisoner at eight ounces. This food, often unhealthy, weakened the men and caused all sorts of illnesses, sometimes with fatal consequences. "There was a guy from the Winnipeg Grenadiers in North Point, a Jew, who got hiccups. He started barking like a dog while dragging himself around the camp. He barked like that for three days and died. He must have suffered a lot. That's the worst thing I saw in that camp."

At the end of September 1942, the Japanese transferred the Canadian prisoners from North Point to Sham Shui Po in the New Territories.

Sham Shui Po had been our army camp when we arrived in Hong Kong. The Japanese had taken everything from the barracks. Only the cement floors were left; there were no windows, no doors, and no beds either. There were already other prisoners when I got to Sham Shui Po. There were British, Indians, Portuguese, Australians, and even a guy who had escaped from Dunkirk and had later been posted to Hong Kong. He told us that Dunkirk was nothing compared to Hong Kong because they had weapons to defend themselves there. In Hong Kong, there were no ships, no planes. We were sixteen thousand prisoners from all nationalities. At noon, the Japanese sent in a truck loaded with rice in old oil barrels. We lined up ten rows on each side of the road and when the truck drove by, they threw shovels of rice on the ground. If a guy was lucky, he could pick up a handful and didn't have to wait until the next day to eat. That's how they fed us.

The Japanese forced us to build an airfield. Our camp was twelve miles away and we had to walk morning and night. We left at six-thirty. A lot of times, we didn't get anything to eat, not even a small bowl of rice, before leaving for work. We hauled gravel on our backs over five miles. We tore down a mountain bigger than the Sugarloaf [at Campbellton] and we carried the rocks for the airport. We also built a small village nearly as big as the town of Bathurst for Kai Tak airport in Kowloon. It wasn't the work that bothered me; it was the food we got and the beatings. We had to be bent over all the time. Your shovel had to move all the time. To carry the rocks and gravel, we had baskets attached to a pole with four ropes. Two guys put the pole on their shoulders and had to run. We couldn't carry it if we walked because it swung from side to side. We had to run five or six miles with up to 200 pounds of rock. My weight was down to 100 pounds by that time.

We left Kai Tak at four or four-thirty in the afternoon but we didn't get to camp until six or seven. Some didn't make it back, they died on the way. If guys fell coming back, they were left there. If they were still there the next day, we picked them up and buried them, six or seven a day. Most of the time, they weren't there because the Chinese had picked them up. We went out in a truck around seven or eight every evening to bury the dead. Those we had buried the evening before were often gone the next day. The Chinese had taken them out of their graves for the wood from the coffins and the cloth which covered the bodies. Sometimes, even the bodies were gone. I don't know if the Chinese ate them or what. When the Japanese saw this, they decided to bury the men naked and without coffins. After that, the Chinese didn't dig up the graves. At North Point and at Sham Shui Po, prisoners who were too sick to work were thrown into a large barrack. You could hear them screaming and moaning. The guys had lost so much weight, their figure changed so much that you didn't recognize them at all.

Sanitary conditions at Sham Shui Po were deplorable. The basic ration, a small quantity of poor-quality rice, caused all sorts of health problems for the POWs. Those, like Pitre, who survived considered themselves lucky.

I caught all sorts of illnesses. I had dysentery. When I ate, it went right through. There was no medicine. All the doctor had was hot water when he was lucky enough to get some. He only had razor blades to operate. If a guy had an infected toe, he cut it off but it never bled and the patient felt no pain at all. My legs swelled up to twice their size and became black. I nearly died. I was suffering from beriberi.[43]

At the beginning of 1943, the Japanese began transferring their prisoners to Japan to work in war industries and mines. This practice was contrary to the Hague Convention, which Japan had signed in 1907.

---

43   Beriberi is an illness caused by the lack of Vitamin B due to eating only husked rice.

Canadian and British doctors tried to save lives in primitive conditions at Sham Shui Po. As this drawing by Lieutenant A.V. Skvorzov entitled "Operating Table" shows, they had only razor blades and knives to operate.

Canadian War Museum/ 19710261-6031

Signatories promised not to force POWs to do work directly related to the war effort. If the conditions were difficult in the camps in Hong Kong, they were doubly so in Japan for Pitre and the others.

They sent us to Japan in April 1943. We were in new barracks at camp 3D in Yokohama [near Tokyo]. They were about 150 feet long and 30 feet wide and were L-shaped. In one corner were the washrooms with a large tub as big as my house and three or four feet deep. They only gave us water for washing in winter. In summer, there was not enough water because it was too hot. In winter, you had to break the ice to get in the tub. There were two-level beds. They were made from boards and the mattresses were pressed straw. They were full of lice and fleas which ate us alive. The floor was coal and we had to sweep it three or four times a day. The camps at North Point and Sham Shui Po were surrounded by electrified barbed wire. In Japan, the fence was of bamboo posts split in two and tied together. The only thing better in Yokohama was the weather. It was more like the temperature here except that it wasn't cold in winter. It only snowed twice while I was there. The first storm was in April. We walked a mile and a half in snow up to our knees. We didn't have any shoes, boots, socks, or pants, just a sort of diaper [a *Fundoshi*, the traditional Japanese loincloth for men].

Some five hundred prisoners from camp 3D worked at the Nippon Kokan shipyard in the Kawasaki district of Yokohama. The treatment of the POWs depended on the humour of those who supervised them. For Pitre, humanitarian sentiments were rare among the Japanese.

I was a riveter. We built warships and large cargo ships. I spent more than two years there. Of all the Japanese I met, I can say I met only one good one. He was the foreman on a ship we were building. He didn't allow my friend and I to work during the last two months we were there. He hid us in a corner; he banged on the ship to make believe we were working. He was a big man, shoulders the width of seven axe handles. When I first saw him, I told my friend we were done for, that he was going to kill us. We spoke enough Japanese to get along with him.

Japanese civilians who worked with us on the ship were always complaining of hunger. Our foreman told us he had killed his eighteen-year-old daughter and that they had eaten her. He cried while telling us what he had done. He wanted his family to survive; he had four or five children. People had little to eat, only two small rice balls per day. On our way to work, I saw women who waited for up to two days in the street for a guy to come with a cart of carrots. They could buy one or two each. Those eight and older couldn't get any bread.

Despite the friendliness of his foreman at the shipyard, Pitre saw no improvement in the food the Japanese gave to POWs.

The food wasn't great. At noon, we got a bowl of hot water. If a horse died, they cooked the hoofs, the head, and the insides, and served it to us. At noon in the shipyard, they put everything in a little dish but we couldn't touch it until the guards told us to eat. They walked by and took a look. If they saw one man had three pieces of meat and another only one, they took a piece and put it on the other guy's plate. If you had a large potato and someone else had three small ones, they cut off a piece of the large one if they thought it was bigger than the three small ones.

Food became a real obsession with the prisoners. Their guards seemed to take pleasure torturing them with the sight of food.

Our camp was about three miles from the shipyard. One evening when coming back to camp, the street was covered with fish for about two hundred feet. It stank like hell! We walked on it for a week on our way to and from work. The guys spat on the fish and all that. One evening when we got to the spot, everything was gone. We told ourselves that the Japanese must have become fed up with the smell. When we got to camp, there was a bag full of fish at each bed. We ate some for three days. It was good because it was dry; the sun had burned it. We weren't too fussy about what we ate. If you saw an animal scurry across the floor, it was who could catch it first.

Unlike prisoners of war held in Germany, who could rely on the regular arrival of Red Cross parcels, those in Japan did not get them often. Their guards were suspicious of these packages that contained things they had never seen.

We only got Red Cross parcels twice. The first time was the evening of New Year's Day in 1944. The packages weighed twelve pounds and we were twelve to a parcel. It was one pound per man. They contained small boxes of butter and a twelve-ounce can of bully beef we divided among four guys. The only things left in the parcels were what the Japanese thought was poisonous.

They were afraid to eat them. I remember going into a Japanese officer's room to bring him hot water to shave. He had a box of Carnation powdered milk and was getting ready to put it on his face. I asked what he was doing. He answered he thought it was shaving soap. It told him it was for drinking and not shaving. He said I was crazy. I took some cold water, put a spoonful of power in the cup and drank it. The officer made me sit down. He called over one of the sergeants and told him what I had done. Both sat down in front of me. They were waiting for me to die. When they saw that I was still alive, they drank the milk.

They were strange people. They didn't want to eat chocolate bars. They took one, broke it in pieces, handed it out, and waited to see if we'd die. When they saw that it didn't kill us, they stopped giving them to us and ate it themselves. The second time we got parcels, a man from the Red Cross entered the camp with them. The Japanese gave them out while he was there. I remember getting a small box of butter which I made last for two weeks. I'd put a bit of butter on my finger and grease my dish. The butter mixed with the rice and I licked the plate for hours.

Most of the guards treated the prisoners with contempt. The slightest gesture on the prisoners' part gave them an excuse to humiliate them. Pitre remembered that it did not take much to arouse their anger.

Everything the guards did made no sense. It was only to make us suffer because they hated White people. They gave us maybe three packs of cigarettes, five cigarettes per pack, during the whole time I was in Japan. They gave them to us and, two or three days later, they came into the hut and asked what we had done with the cigarettes. They punished us when we said we had smoked them. They sent us outside in the middle of winter, the five hundred of us, and forced each one to rub his body with his little diaper. When we were done, the Japanese moved on to the next one until the five hundred men had done the same thing.

They gave us ashtrays, the bottoms of tin cans. Everyone who smoked had to put his elbows on the table with the ashtray right in front of him. If they caught one without it, they took everybody outside and forced him to shake hands with the others and apologize for having smoked without an ashtray. It wasn't enough to apologize, because we had to make a long story about where the cigarettes came from and all that. We spent the night outside. Next morning, they sent us out to work without breakfast. If you had the misfortune to break the little dish in which you ate, it was the same damn thing: everyone outside and you had to explain how it happened. We spent some awful evenings.

After three years in Japanese hands, the prisoners were weak from malnutrition and disease. One might have thought that the detainees benefited from better medical care since they were near the large hospitals in Tokyo. Pitre remembered that the sick and wounded just disappeared.

I saw a man, Sergeant Cole,[44] who became terribly swollen. His body was all black. They operated on him [in the camp]. His flesh was black and thick but not a drop of blood came out. It was so rotten that they couldn't sew the incision back together. He died like that. His son was also there but he survived. Many died from dysentery in our camp. The Japanese took three or four men to hospital in Tokyo. We never saw them after that. One of my friends from the Winnipeg Grenadiers was injured when a piece of steel fell on his leg. It was split open from the knee to the groin. I could see the bone and the nerves but it never bled a drop. He didn't feel any pain. We put him in a wheelbarrow and took him to hospital in Tokyo, about three miles from the shipyard. I never saw him after that.

---

44   Sergeant Elmer Cole of the Royal Rifles, from Sussex, New Brunswick, died on March 16, 1944. He was forty-five years old. His twenty-one-year-old son Bliss served in the same regiment.

For many prisoners, death seemed to be the only true escape. Others obviously thought of trying to escape the hell of the camp. It was probably with a certain fatalism that some acted on their plans. "The evening of New Year's in 1944, a man from the Winnipegs escaped. The Japanese soldiers didn't even go out to hunt him down. Civilians brought him back to camp three or four hours later. The guards tied him to a post near the gate and left him there. He froze to death. It wasn't worth while trying to escape because a White person among Japanese didn't go unnoticed."

The Japanese were unable to break the spirit of resistance of the Canadian POWs despite all the mistreatment. They took revenge on what had become the symbol of their enslavement, the Nippon Kokan shipyard. "The only time we had time off was when things went terribly wrong at work. We set fire to a building in the yard. We didn't go to work for three days. They didn't want us to see the damage. We returned on the fourth day and found they had hidden everything behind a wall ten feet high. We knew what had happened because we were the ones who had set the fire."[45]

By the spring of 1945, the war was ending in Europe, but in the Pacific the Japanese fiercely resisted American and other Allied forces approaching their country. The conflict in the Pacific differed greatly from the one in Europe because here the Allies could advance only by capturing numerous occupied islands that allowed American bombers to attack Japan itself. On the morning of March 9, 1945, some 334 B-29 bombers dropped tons of incendiary bombs on Tokyo. Most of the buildings were built of wood, and 20 percent of the capital was destroyed, with about 130,000 killed or injured. From camp 3D, the prisoners could see the clouds of smoke over Tokyo. This scene warmed their hearts because they saw a concrete sign that the winds of war were turning against Japan. Pitre heard good news in early May on what was a special day for him. "On May 7, I was riveting under a ship when a Japanese came to tell us that the war with Germany was over. It was my birthday; I was twenty-five

---

45   Two Canadians, Sergeant Charlie Clark and Private Ken Cameron, set the fire on January 18, 1944.

years old on that day. We were sent to work in coal mines in northern Japan shortly after."

When he left the Nippon Kokan shipyard, Pitre lost the foreman who had become a sort of protector. Conditions for POWs deteriorated as the war progressed to the detriment of the Japanese.

The camps in northern Japan were the worst. They were just good enough for animals. The barracks didn't have floors. They were made of bamboo and newsprint. It was like hell in those mines. We went under a mountain about a mile and a half and turned to go three miles under the sea. It was so hot in the mine that in some places the water was hot enough to make tea. You couldn't put your hand in it because it was so hot. There were two shafts. They took out rock from one and coal from the other. It was very cold in the one where the rock was coming out. We couldn't go through that one because we didn't have any clothes, only our little diaper.

We went down, about fifty of us, about a mile and a half on a little trolley, then walked about a mile to take another [trolley] to the coal face. There we began hacking away and digging for coal. There were three eight-hour shifts. We had a quota of coal to get out. If a group didn't reach its quota, we had to stay there until it was out. Some guys had to work two shifts. It was hard. We could be six men in a gallery half a mile from another group because we were not all together. There was a large junction with about twenty-five lines where a man operated a winch. I did that for a while. The small coal wagons arrived at the junction and were all put on the same track. When all the wagons were there, I signalled the guy up on top. He pulled it up. Other prisoners worked above unloading them. If they saw American planes on their way to bomb, they'd write an X on the box. That's how we knew there were bombings.

Freed Allied prisoners of war in Yokohama, Japan, September 1945.
They were given food and new clothes before being sent home. LAC / 3403250

The end of their enslavement came without warning. In the camp and in the mine, they were without news of the events taking place elsewhere in Japan. American bombers passing over the camp was a clear sign that the defeat of Japan was only a question of time. On August 6, 1945, a B-29, the "Enola Gay," dropped an atom bomb on Hiroshima. Three days later, another B-29, the "Great Artist," dropped a bomb on Nagasaki in southern Japan, finally convincing Emperor Hirohito to accept Japan's unconditional surrender.

Pitre's last hours in captivity were nearly his last on Earth.

We were underground the night the Americans dropped the atom bomb [on Nagasaki]. The power went out. We had to walk up to get out of the mine. When we began making our way out, we nearly drowned because the water started to rise since the pumps didn't work. We had water up to our armpits. That lasted about twenty minutes before the water rushed by carrying pieces of wood, stones, and coal. When we got to the top, not one Japanese was around. We went to our barrack and asked the doctor what was going on. He said he didn't know but that all the guards had left when the lights went out.

Even if the prisoners suspected the war was over, they only learned of the surrender the next day. For Pitre, it was the end of forty-four months of hell and humiliation.

Next morning, around seven, three small planes from an American aircraft carrier flew over the camp and dropped a carton of cigarettes, a newspaper, and a note saying the war was over. The note also said they'd come back in half an hour to bring us food. When we learned the war was over, we were like a bunch of kids who had never gotten a gift in their lives and who, all of a sudden, were getting a whole lot. We didn't know what to do, what to say. Guys were sitting down and many were crying. Half an hour later, four or five of those small planes came and dropped enough food for our breakfast. They came at noon every day after that and dropped our meal. On the third day, sixteen big aircraft, B-29s, dropped at least fifteen carloads of food. There was enough to feed four armies. There must have been 500 pounds of chocolate on my bed when I left camp. Everything stayed there. I have never seen so much food in all my life. They dropped everything except for a woman. There were movies, clothes, everything.... Nothing was missing.

MacArthur[46] spoke on the radio to tell us the war was over and that we could take what we wanted from the Japanese. When the

---

46   General Douglas MacArthur, Commander-in-Chief, US Army Forces Pacific.

guys heard this, they went to the city two miles from the camp. Guys who hadn't walked for four years went out on all fours. We had been asked to stay where we were because it would be easier for the Americans to find us than for us to find them. We went to the train station and took a train. The Japanese took us to Tokyo. The Americans were there when we arrived. We boarded the *Missouri*, the ship on which the surrender had been signed [on September 2, 1945]. We spent three days in the ship's hospital before being taken to the airport on the other side of Yokohama. We were flown to San Francisco via Iwo Jima, Guam, Johnston Island, and Hawaii. We stopped everywhere for two or three days to get medical care. We didn't eat at all, we took vitamins. From San Francisco, we headed to Vancouver by train.

Pitre's return to Canada didn't mean an end to his suffering. "At the beginning, I weighed 150 pounds and I was in good shape. At the end, I was down to 75 pounds. For the first six months I was home, I drank a powder the Red Cross gave me. I must have drunk twenty gallons. I spent nearly three years in hospitals in Sussex and Saint John. I went for two or three weeks, stayed home for two or three weeks, before going back to hospital." Pitre gained weight in the years following the war, but health problems resulting from his imprisonment lasted long after his return.

His suffering during those four years was not only physical. He was not about to forget the humiliation he suffered at the hands of the Japanese or forgive them for the torment they caused him.

With all the suffering I went through, it's funny but I never thought of home. It was like a dream. I always told myself that I wouldn't come out alive and that it was better to forget everything. We often got letters from home. The Japanese made us go outside, threw them on the ground, poured oil on them, and burned them. We didn't have any news from home at all. There was no difference in the way we were treated from the first to the last day. It was always the same damn thing: a beating every day.

If you did something, they punished you. They'd put a load of bricks on your back and make you crawl on all fours around the grounds. If you didn't bow low enough for an officer, they made you bow quickly. They were evil. I still hate the Japanese.... It's the same today as the day I was captured. It's still all in my head. When I go to bed at night and close my eyes, I still see all that. It's something I can't forget. Seeing men die and suffering from hunger, it's sad.[47]

The Japanese were not the only ones Léo Pitre and many Hong Kong veterans have not forgiven. "Our government dealt us a low blow. When we left Hawaii for Hong Kong, there was a ship following us with tanks, trucks, and munitions. The Canadian government had it turn around and come back to Canada. It could have done the same with us…"

Pitre worked at the pulp and paper mill in Bathurst for two years after his return home. He later worked in construction all over New Brunswick. He married Joséphine Pitre in 1947. They had four children and they lived in Bathurst.

---

47   Some 260 Canadian soldiers captured at Hong Kong died in POW camps.

Chapter Eleven

"They wanted to humiliate us"
The Story of Guy Sirois

Many other Acadians served in the Far East. Among them was Guy Sirois.
It was because he dreamed of travelling, of seeing the world, that Sirois
volunteered for the army on August 10, 1940. The young man from Saint-
Hilaire in northwest New Brunswick was twenty-three years old. For
the past three years he had worked on road construction for the Dexter
Company.

> I left my job at noon on Saturday and went to enlist right away at
> the old post office in Edmundston. I wanted to join the Carleton
> and York but there was no more room. There wasn't any in the
> Fusiliers de Sherbrooke either. There was a captain from the
> Royal Rifles who was recruiting. I joined them because I wanted
> to be in the army. I was young and wanted to travel. I didn't think
> about the war.

It was as a rifleman with an infantry regiment from Quebec City that
Sirois's dream became a reality. Later, however, the dream would become
a nightmare, one that began on Christmas Day 1941 in Hong Kong and
ended in Niigata, Japan in mid-August 1945.

Men of C Company, The Royal Rifles of Canada,
disembarking at Hong Kong, November 16, 1941. LAC / PA-037419

After training in Valcartier, Quebec, the Royal Rifles were sent to Newfoundland to do guard duty. After returning to Valcartier, they were sent to Vancouver.

When we boarded the ship [*Awatea*] in Vancouver, we didn't know where we were going. There were rumours that we were heading to Jamaica or to Singapore. Only the officers knew we were going to Hong Kong. We left near the end of October [October 27]. It took us twenty-one days. We stopped in Hawaii and Manila in the Philippines but didn't have the right to get off the ship.

The two Canadian regiments landing in Hong Kong in mid-November, The Royal Rifles of Canada and The Winnipeg Grenadiers, were not trained for combat, having served as garrison troops in Newfoundland and Jamaica before crossing to Asia. "We did guard duty. It was the same thing we had done in Newfoundland. Each company did guard duty for a week." Military and civilian leaders in Hong Kong knew that the Japanese army was near the colony in the Chinese province of Guangdong. What they did not know was that the commander of Japanese forces had already received his orders to prepare an assault on Hong Kong. He was waiting for the green light from Tokyo. By early December, more than fifty thousand men of the 38th Japanese Infantry Division had advanced to a start line under cover of darkness. Unlike the defenders of Hong Kong, left without the possibility of reinforcement in case of attack, the Japanese could rely on thousands of other troops already in occupied China.

Our company, B Company, was on guard duty in the mountains around Mount Stanley. We were to return to our barracks in Kowloon on December 7, but were told to stay in our positions because the Japanese had just attacked Pearl Harbor. We weren't trained for combat. We weren't ready. The Japanese had been fighting in China for many years, and the British didn't think the Japanese would attack. The Japanese began bombing on

December 8. The first thing they struck was the airport. They destroyed the few British planes that were there. After that they could come down and bomb as they wanted. They bombed us for ten days. It was without letup, day and night. After that, they landed on Hong Kong Island [on December 18]. They attacked in force, and we didn't have a choice but to retreat. We had no possibility of advancing. We were about fourteen thousand in all, with the navy and the air force. The Japanese must have been two hundred thousand or more. When we lost a man, we had nobody to replace him. We had no reinforcements or other help. If we killed two Japanese, ten came up; if we killed ten, twenty showed up. We had to fight to the bitter end.

The day before the surrender, we were on a mountain. That's where they killed my lieutenant and the sergeant manning the machine gun for our platoon. We were forced to retreat. We backed up and backed up until we had both feet in the water on the other side of the island. That's when the general [Major-General C.M. Maltby] decided to surrender to the Japanese. We spent Christmas Day waiting and backing up. On the twenty-sixth, we were told the general had called the governor [Sir Mark Young] to inform him that resistance was impossible and that we had to surrender. They raised the white flag. We were told to disarm. We put all our arms in a garage: guns, munitions, grenades, et cetera. We waited there for three days. We didn't see many Japanese, only an officer once in a while who showed up at camp. On the fourth day, they made us go down to North Point, which had been a refugee camp. We walked twelve miles.

It was at North Point that Sirois and other Canadians began to realize that their captivity would not be a holiday. The conditions in the camp at the time were relatively good compared to what awaited them in other POW camps later on.

When we got to North Point, we saw that it was dirty, really filthy. I think the Japanese had used the camp as a stable. We cleaned it up a bit. We hadn't eaten much for the last three days because our army rations didn't get to us all the time. The Japanese took all the army provisions — there was enough for three months — and began giving us rice, and only rice. The Japanese confiscated all our medical supplies. I remember that Canadian doctors had to operate on a guy suffering from appendicitis. The only thing they had was peanut oil and salt. Even that was scarce. We only worked for two or three weeks at the beginning. We spent our time playing softball.

The time for sports quickly ended when the Japanese decided to transfer them to another camp and exploit their labour.

After some time, we were sent to Sham Shui Po. The Japanese forced us to build Kai Tak airport. We tore down a mountain with picks and shovels to build the airport. The work was quite hard but, at the time, we were not yet in too bad a shape. We transported sand in wheelbarrows. We spread it out and poured cement for the landing strips. The days were not bad even if the Japanese pushed us a bit, but they weren't too brutal yet. The camp was hit by a diphtheria epidemic which lasted quite a while. Up to five or six guys could die in a day. We were about forty soldiers who had given their names to work in the hospital to help the doctors. We worked as orderlies but we weren't nurses. We went to fetch water and things like that. Not one of the forty men caught diphtheria. When I was captured, I weighed between 160 and 165 pounds. I had lost about twenty pounds but was still in pretty good shape.

The landing strips and the building at Kai Tak completed, the prisoners were of no more value in Hong Kong. That is when the Japanese decided to use their labour in war industries in Japan. The first Canadians left Sham Shui Po in January 1943. Sirois and hundreds of others

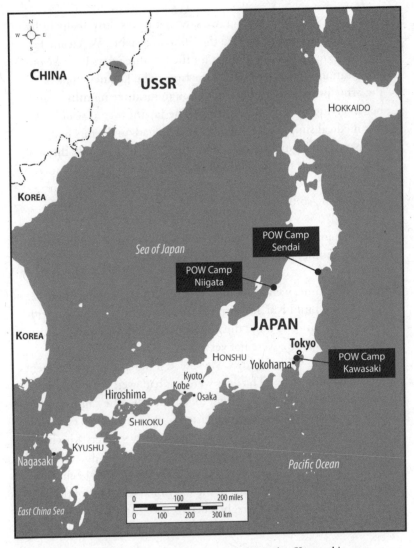

Three of the POW camps in Japan were located at Kawasaki, near
Yokohama (Camp 3D), and at Sendai and Niigata, north of Tokyo.
Atom bombs were dropped on Hiroshima and Nagasaki in August 1945.

Ronald Cormier / Mike Bechthold

followed later. It was the beginning of an infernal voyage. The men were crammed like livestock into the holds of merchant ships. They had little to eat. There was no ventilation and no toilets in the holds. Most of the prisoners suffered from seasickness or dysentery. They were unrecognizable when they disembarked in Japan. They had spent days at sea, and were dirty and covered in excrement.

Our company crossed in October 1943. We were sent to Niigata in the north of the country. In winter, the snow lasted two months. The barracks were from 18 to 20 feet wide and 100 to 125 feet long. We slept on wooden boards and had only a small blanket. It was cold and humid in Niigata in winter. You went to bed all dressed under your small blanket and you didn't want to get out. There was no heat in the barracks. We were thin and didn't have much energy to burn. The roof of the barracks was made of bamboo. The roof of one collapsed under the weight of the snow one winter. Seven or eight prisoners were killed. The camp was surrounded by barbed wire eight to ten feet tall. We didn't have the strength to climb over it because we didn't have enough energy to step over the threshold of our barrack. They electrified the fence after a while. One day a dog got too close to it and its tail hit the fence. The dog fell dead. There was a small lower fence in front of the electrified one. We didn't have the right to go farther than that.

We got up between four-thirty and five in the morning. We had to do half an hour's physical exercises before breakfast...a small bowl of rice. The exercises were compulsory. I had a hard time lifting my feet. After breakfast we walked to the foundry where we worked. It was about three miles from camp. We walked morning and night. They brought our dinner there...a bowl of rice. We worked eight to ten hours a day. We came back around eight in the evening but we didn't have the right to go to bed before nine. We had one day off a week, always on Monday, never on Sunday. At the foundry where I worked, we built engines for submarines. Our officers protested because the Japanese didn't have the right to force prisoners to work in war industries. The Japanese claimed they were commercial engines. They were the ones running things.

We didn't have any contact with Japanese civilians who worked there because they didn't understand us and we didn't have the right to talk to them. Some women were making engine moulds. One evening, one approached me and said "*Wifo?*" She wanted to know if I was married. I replied "No." Our foremen, all civilians, walked around with clubs in their hands to show their authority. If you didn't do what you were supposed to, they hit you on the back with the club. One time, the Japanese made us walk twelve miles, about forty of us, to get oxygen tanks needed to cut iron. We hung them around our necks and walked to Niigata in snow up to the crotch. We were nothing more than horses for them. We had to bow down to officers in camp. We nearly had to crawl before them. They felt terribly superior. They wanted to humiliate us, to degrade White people.

The goal of the Japanese was to break the morale of the POWs by humiliating them. They were sometimes successful, but the survival instincts of most of the victims of brutality helped them to overcome adversity, as Sirois remembered.

We couldn't let ourselves go, get discouraged. A guy came to work with us one day at the foundry. After getting back to the barrack that evening, he told us he was fed up, that he'd had enough. He was dead the next morning.[48] We were five guys from Edmundston in Niigata. There was Bob Jessop and his brother, Albert, Algée Pelletier, T.M. Richards, and myself. Richards died at the end of 1943 or early 1944. He was older than me, he was thirty-four or thirty-five. I think T.M. gave up and he let himself

---

48   Of the 1,184 Canadians who were prisoners of war in Japan, 136 did not survive.

die.[49] I was ill for four or five months. I had a hard time getting up. I was suffering from beriberi and dysentery. My feet were swollen and I had a hard time walking. My determination got me through that. We were treated like slaves, not like prisoners of war. They beat us two or three times a week. You had to bow your head and endure what they did to you. What was hardest was not being able to take revenge. They had rifles, we only had shovels.

Hunger dominated life in the camps.

Our ration was rice with greens three times a day. We never had enough. Ten minutes after eating your ration, you could have eaten another one. It didn't sustain us. That was our diet during the whole time I was a prisoner of war... rice, rice, and more rice. When you went to work in the morning and you saw an apple core on the road, you grabbed it. Those who have not known hunger can't imagine what it's like. We had so little to eat that some even ate rats. They caught them, killed them, skinned them, and boiled them. One had to be quite low to do that. I never ate any. I couldn't have, I would have died first. The doctors told them not to eat rats because they lived in the sewers. I had little energy at the end. I weighed less than eighty pounds.

We got five or six parcels from the Red Cross while in Japan. We sometimes shared one among four guys. They once offered us a parcel for eight prisoners but we refused. We tried to make it last as long as possible but it was hard. Our doctors warned us not to eat too much at once because our stomachs couldn't resist. After the war, we heard stories of men who died because they ate everything at once. There were packs of cigarettes in the Red Cross parcels. We traded them with Japanese guards from time to time, a pack of Canadian ones for three Japanese. The Japanese cigarettes were unsmokable; they tasted like straw.

---

49   Sergeant Thomas Medley Richards died on February 13, 1944; he was forty-three years old.

The Canadians quickly realized that they would be behind barbed wire until the end of the war. They knew they were at a disadvantage because of their recent arrival in Hong Kong. Sirois and most of the other POWs took the threat against those who tried to escape seriously.

It was impossible to try to escape because we were on an island. The idea never even came to me while we were in Kowloon. A few Brits escaped from Kowloon. They had been in Hong Kong for years, spoke Chinese, and knew the area well. After that, the Japanese gathered us in groups of five and told us they'd kill all the men in the same room if one escaped. Our officers ordered us not to try because we'd have lost too many men. Four Canadians tried to escape in Japan. The Japanese caught them the next day and executed them.

Escape meant certain death for those who were fed up with the cruelty of their Japanese masters. Only the end of the war would bring liberation for some twelve hundred Canadians held in camps in Japan and about four hundred others still in Hong Kong in the summer of 1945. These men had had no contact with their families and no official news of what was happening outside the camp. They were hopeful that the Allies would defeat Japan. "I only had news from my parents once, but it didn't come directly from them. I got a letter from Énoïl Michaud, who was Minister of Justice in Ottawa.[50] There were only two lines that said my father and mother were well. I wrote once but my parents never got the letter."

The end of the war came without notice in Niigata and the other camps. The prisoners did not understand what was happening.

I was liberated in mid-August. On the Tuesday [the fourteenth] following our Monday off, we didn't go to work. It was the same on Wednesday. We were wondering what was going on. The Japanese circulated the news that there was no steel for the

---

50   J. Énoïl Michaud was the Member of Parliament for Madawaska, and served as interim Minister of Justice.

foundry because the ship hadn't come in. Four days later they told us the war was over. It was "Hip, hip, hip, hurrah!" We even stopped eating rice. American planes dropped food in fifty-gallon drums. There was chocolate and rich food. We had to be careful what we ate because our stomachs had shrunk. The guards left after four days. Only a few officers were there to stop civilians from coming into the camp. They warned us not to go out before August 26 because they were afraid of civilians attacking us. But there was no danger from civilians. After our liberation, we went out and met civilians. They shook our hands. They were happy the war was over. They were sorry for what Japan had done. Even the soldiers were glad the war had ended. The Japanese finally told us that the Americans had dropped bombs that had destroyed Hiroshima and Nagasaki. They didn't know they were atom bombs. It's only when the Americans came to get us that we learned what they were.

The newly freed prisoners did not have time to feel sorry for the victims of Hiroshima and Nagasaki. After 1,330 days of captivity and brutality, they thought only of going home and getting on with their lives.

We left Japan in early September. Our ship stopped in Guam and Honolulu on its way to San Francisco. From there, we took the train to Vancouver. After two days in Vancouver, I took the train for home. My parents had only learned in the fall of 1942 that I was alive and a POW. They had heard on radio that Hong Kong had fallen, but didn't know what had happened to me. I thought I was going to surprise my family, but, when I left Vancouver, the Red Cross began sending them telegrams saying where I was and how I was doing. It was two-thirty in the morning when I arrived in Saint-Hilaire [at the end of November 1945]. All of my family was waiting for me. I was the one who was surprised.

Liberated Canadian POWs from Japan arriving in Vancouver, October 1945. LAC / PA-116797

The three years and eight months of imprisonment left their mark on Sirois. Although his health had improved since his liberation, military authorities felt he still needed care to return to a normal life. "The guys from Edmundston were called to hospital in Sussex in early December. We told them we'd go if we got leave for Christmas. After two weeks of treatments in Sussex, we went home for Christmas. We returned to the hospital after the holidays. I stayed there until my demobilization in June 1946."

Half a century after the events, Sirois bore no rancour against those who sent him to Hong Kong or those who mistreated him, but he had never understood the reasons for his presence in Hong Kong, half a world away. "When we went over, the government knew it wasn't possible to reinforce or defend Hong Kong. I don't know why they sent us. I bear no grudge against the Canadian government or the Japanese. It was war. We were simply unlucky. Most of us thought the war would be over in a year when we were captured. Nobody expected it to last four years."

Guy Sirois had joined the army to travel. He could not have imagined the terrible personal cost of his trip through hell. In 1946, he married Yolande Bossé; they had three children. He worked for the provincial Department of Highways in Edmundston for nearly thirty years, and retired in 1976. The couple lived in Edmundston.

Conclusion

The men in this book represent those young Acadians who served their country during the Second World War. Most were still in their teens or barely out of them. They left everything behind and embarked on an uncertain journey without knowing if they would survive. Those who returned were profoundly changed. Their memories of events grew fainter with the years and ultimately followed them to the grave. They all experienced the horrors and cruelty of war in different ways. Men who served in bombers with the RCAF or the RAF lived moments of intense terror in the air. Their reward if they returned was to sleep in a clean bed in a heated building. If they were shot down, death or imprisonment awaited them.

Things were different for the men on the ground. They engaged the enemy sometimes for days on end, often without letup. Their proximity to the enemy also meant they could be killed or captured at any moment. Those who became prisoners were at the mercy of their captors and were deprived of their freedom and dignity.

Acadians were frowned upon by the anglophone majority for having opposed conscription for overseas service. They equated it with refusal to serve. Nevertheless, thousands of young Acadians volunteered for service abroad, and the vast majority of them served in units where things were done in English. Veteran Joseph LeBouthillier recalled that "about forty of us joined up on the same day in Bathurst from down here [the Caraquet region] who didn't know a word of English. We had a hard time understanding and being understood."[51] They were francophones, but accepted that they were in the minority. There were few conflicts because of language, and they soon learned English. The men realized that their lives in combat depended on others regardless of the language spoken. Acadians became valuable assets when, in 1944, the Allies landed in Normandy, where they were able to gather information from French citizens on enemy positions and minefields.

Most young Acadians who went off to war between 1939 and 1945 came from rural communities. When they came home, there were few parades to welcome them. They felt that their sacrifice was unappreciated. Those who had stayed home did not want to hear about their experiences in combat. When they volunteered, they were promised good jobs, but most of them had a hard time finding work afterwards. As Joseph LeBouthillier remembered, most were "returned to civilian life like a pig in a poke."[52]

Many Acadian veterans later became leaders in their regions. With the passage of time, they saw that anglophone communities honoured veterans, and realized that they were not less worthy. Yet it took many long years before their sacrifice was recognized. Many English-speaking villages and towns had erected cenotaphs after the First World War, but there were few in Acadian rural areas. It was only in the 1960s that memorials began to be built to honour them: among others, in Memramcook in 1966, Cap-Pelé in 1970, and Neguac in 1972. Even Dieppe, which was renamed to remember the Canadian sacrifice of August 19, 1942, did not have a cenotaph until 1981.

It is, however, as heroes that we must remember them in our collective memory. We have a DUTY TO REMEMBER.

---

51   Joseph LeBouthillier, quoted in *Forgotten Soldiers*, 87.
52   Ibid., 97.

Acknowledgements

It is hard to believe that it has taken me more than twenty-five years to have an English-language adaptation of my book, *Entre bombes et barbelés*, become a reality. In the early 1990s, I approached numerous publishers, but they were not interested in the project. In one way, this was fortunate because it allowed me to add much new information as well as a new chapter to the original version.

In April 2021, I approached Marc Milner of the Gregg Centre for the Study of War and Society, and informed him that I was interested in having *Bombs and Barbed Wire* published. He told me about the book series of the New Brunswick Military Heritage Project (NBMHP) and asked that I send him an outline and a few chapters, which he would pass on to Brent Wilson, director of the NBMHP. Brent was quick to respond, and he began to edit and make suggestions within a few weeks. By mid-July, the editorial committee had approved the project and the real work of finalizing the manuscript began in earnest.

I am grateful to Brent for all his comments, which made the stories more informative. I also wish to thank copy editor Barry Norris and proofreaders Noeline Bridge and Clarissa Hurley for their work on the book. Thank you to Alan Sheppard, production editor at Goose Lane Editions, for all his assistance in preparing the book for publishing; to Julie Scriver for layout; and to Mike Bechthold for reworking the maps.

I am forever thankful to the men in this book who told me their stories for posterity. Some of their children had never heard their fathers talk about their war experiences. I also thank family members who provided me with new information and provided photos.

Selected Bibliography

Primary Sources

Unpublished Documents

Dubé, Henri Édouard, Service file of Canadian war dead, 1939-1947, Library and Archives Canada, Ottawa, series RG 24, volume 27417, 315 pages.

Historical summary, No. 142 Royal Air Force Squadron, provided to the author by the Air Historical Branch, UK Ministry of Defence, London.

Other Primary Sources

Telephone conversation and email with Daniel Servais, former mayor of Olizy-Primat, France.

Secondary Sources

Abautret, René. *Dieppe, le sacrifice des Canadiens*. Paris: Cercle du livre de France / Robert Lafont, 1969.

Bailey, Ronald H. *Prisoners of War*. Alexandria, VA: Time-Life Books, 1981.

Barker, Ralph. *The 1,000 Plan*. London: Pan Books, 1965.

Bennett, D.C.T. *Pathfinder*. London: Sphere Books, 1958.

Bowman, Martin W. *We Were Eagles: The Eight Air Force at War*, vol. 3. Gloucestershire, UK: Ambley Publishing, 2015.

Calin, Harold. *Dieppe*. New York: Tower, 1978.

Cent ans d'histoire d'un régiment canadien-français, les Fusiliers Mont-Royal, 1869-1969. Montreal: Éditions du Jour, 1971.

Dancocks, Daniel G. *In Enemy Hands*. Edmonton: Hurtig Publishers, 1983.

Douglas, W.A.B., and Brereton Greenhous. *Out of the Shadows: Canada in the Second World War*. Toronto: Oxford University Press, 1988.

Durand, Arthur A. *Stalag Luft III*. New York: Louisiana State University Press / Simon & Schuster, 1988.

Galante, Pierre. *Operation Valkyrie: The German Generals' Plot against Hitler*. New York: Dell, 1981.

Granatstein, J.L., and Desmond Morton. *Bloody Victory*. Toronto: Lester & Orpen Dennys, 1984.

Kostenuk, Samuel, and John Griffin. *RCAF Squadron Histories and Aircraft 1924-1968*. Toronto: A.M. Kakkert, 1977.

Lindsay, Oliver. *The Lasting Honour*. London: Sphere Books, 1978.

Maguire, Eric. *Dieppe August 19*. London: Corgi Books, 1963.

Mellor, John. *Dieppe, Canada's Forgotten Heroes*. Agincourt, ON: Signet, 1975.

Middlebrook, Martin, and Chris Everitt. *The Bomber Command War Diaries: An Operational Reference Book: 1939-1945*. London: Penguin Books, 1985.

Mordal, Jacques. *Dieppe, The Dawn of Decision*. London: New English Library, 1963.

Nicholson, G.W.L. *The Official History of the Canadian Army in the Second World War: The Canadian Army in Italy, 1943-1945*, vol. 2. Ottawa: Queen's Printer, 1956.

Nolan, Brian. *Hero, the Buzz Beurling Story*. Markham, ON: Penguin Books, 1981.

Potter, John Deane. *Fiasco: The Break-out of the German Battleships*. London: Pan Books, 1970.

Reader's Digest. *The Canadians at War 1939/45*, vols. 1 and 2. Montreal: Reader's Digest Association (Canada), 1969.

Roberts, Leslie. *There Shall Be Wings*. Toronto: Clarke, Irwin, 1959.

Roy, Reginald H. *Débarquement et offensive des Canadiens en Normandie*. Saint-Laurent, QC: Éditions du Trécarré, 1984.

Salmaggi, Cesare, and Alfredo Pallavisini. *2194 Days of War*. New York: Mayflower Books, 1979.

Shores, Christopher. *History of the Royal Canadian Air Force*. Greenwich, CT: Bison Books, 1984.

Simmons, Kenneth W. *Prisoner of War*. Toronto: Bantam Books, 1960.

St. Clair, A.D. (Sandy). *The Endless War*. North Battleford, SK: Turner-Warwick Publications, 1987.

Stacey, C.P. *Official History of the Canadian Army in the Second World War: Six Years of War*, vol. 1. Ottawa: Queen's Printer, 1955.

———. *Official History of the Canadian Army: The Victory Campaign*, vol. 3. Ottawa: Queen's Printer, 1960.

Terraine, John. *The Right of the Line: The Royal Air Force in the European War 1939-1945*. London: Hodder & Stoughton, 1985.

Thompson, R.W. *Dieppe at Dawn*. London: White Lion, 1956.

Toliver, Raymond F. *Nazi Interrogator*. New York: Zebra Books, 1978.

Wheeler, Keith. *Bombers over Japan*. Alexandria, VA: Time-Life Books, 1982.

———. *The Fall of Japan*. Alexandria, VA: Time-Life Books, 1983.

Whitaker, Denis, and Shelagh Whitaker. *Dieppe: Tragedy to Triumph*. Whitby, ON: McGraw-Hill Ryerson, 1992.

Zich, Arthur. *The Rising Sun*. Alexandria, VA: Time-Life Books, 1977.

Newspapers and Periodicals

Commemorative brochure, 50th Anniversary of the Dieppe Raid, August 19, 1942, Ottawa: Veterans Affairs Canada, 1992.

L'Évangéline, May 10, 1945, Moncton.

Legion Magazine, June 1985, Ottawa.

Index

The New Brunswick Military Heritage Project

The New Brunswick Military Heritage Project, a non-profit organization devoted to public awareness of the remarkable military heritage of the province, is an initiative of the Brigadier Milton F. Gregg, VC, Centre for the Study of War and Society of the University of New Brunswick. The organization consists of museum professionals, teachers, university professors, graduate students, active and retired members of the Canadian Forces, and other historians. We welcome public involvement. People who have ideas for books or information for our database can contact us through our website: www.unb.ca/nbmhp.

One of the main activities of the New Brunswick Military Heritage Project is the publication of the New Brunswick Military Heritage Series with Goose Lane Editions. This series of books is under the direction of J. Brent Wilson, Director of the New Brunswick Military Heritage Project at the University of New Brunswick. Publication of the series is supported by a grant from the Province of New Brunswick and the Canadian War Museum.

The New Brunswick Military History Series

Volume 1
Saint John Fortifications, 1630-1956,
Roger Sarty and Doug Knight

Volume 2
*Hope Restored: The American Revolution and the
Founding of New Brunswick,* Robert L. Dallison

Volume 3
The Siege of Fort Beauséjour, 1755, Chris M. Hand

Volume 4 ·
*Riding into War: The Memoir of a Horse Transport Driver,
1916-1919,* James Robert Johnston

Volume 5
*The Road to Canada: The Grand Communications Route
from Saint John to Quebec,* W.E. (Gary) Campbell

Volume 6
*Trimming Yankee Sails: Pirates and Privateers
of New Brunswick,* Faye Kert

Volume 7
*War on the Home Front: The Farm Diaries
of Daniel MacMillan, 1914-1927,*
edited by Bill Parenteau and Stephen Dutcher

About the Author

A resident of Dieppe, New Brunswick, Ronald Cormier is the author of *J'ai vécu la guerre* (published in English as *The Forgotten Soldiers*), *Entre bombes et barbelés*, *Les Acadiens et la Seconde Guerre mondiale*, and *Bombs and Barbed Wire*. Cormier worked as a television producer in news and current affairs with Radio-Canada in Moncton before writing and directing four episodes of *Turning Points of History* for History Television about the Second World War and Korean War.

Cormier is the historian of the Dieppe Military Veterans' Association and has attended dozens of commemorative ceremonies in France for the D-Day Landings and the Dieppe Raid. He has also given numerous presentations in France and Canada on the role Canadians played on D-Day and the liberation of France and Western Europe.